Regional Coopera[...]
Peace and Develop[...]

M000309740

Faced with significant security challenges, in recent years Japan and South Korea have both sought to raise their international profile through peacebuilding, development, humanitarian assistance, and human security. This book assesses the past, present, and future potential of these niche diplomacy initiatives undertaken by Japan and South Korea, largely in Southeast Asia. The book concludes that not only do such nontraditional security channels have the potential to achieve meaningful change for partners and beneficiaries, but they could also form the basis of future confidence-building and security cooperation between Japan and South Korea, which have to date achieved little in the field of traditional security cooperation, despite facing many shared challenges.

Working across disciplines and national boundaries, the contributors to this volume argue that policy prioritization in the fields of peacebuilding, development, and human security by Tokyo and Seoul could have the potential to accrue wider benefits not only to the Northeast Asian actors and the Southeast Asian partners, but also to wider regional and even global security communities. At a time when the role of so-called middle powers is receiving increasing levels of attention both domestically and internationally, this book will be of considerable interest to scholars of Japan and the ROK, as well as development, security, and foreign policy researchers more broadly.

Brendan Howe is Associate Dean of the Graduate School of International Studies, and Director of the Institute for International Trade and Cooperation, at Ewha Womans University, South Korea.

Routledge Research on Asian Development

Development and Gender Capital in India
Change, Continuity and Conflict in Kerala
Shoba Arun

Bangladesh's Graduation from the Least Developed Countries Group
Pitfalls and Promises
Edited by Debapriya Bhattacharya

Regional Cooperation for Peace and Development
Japan and South Korea in Southeast Asia
Edited by Brendan Howe

For more information about this series, please visit: www.routledge.com/Routledge-Research-on-Asian-Development/book-series/RRASIADEV

Regional Cooperation for Peace and Development

Japan and South Korea
in Southeast Asia

Edited by Brendan Howe

Routledge
Taylor & Francis Group

LONDON AND NEW YORK

First published 2019
byRoutledge
2 Park Square, Milton Park, Abingdon, Oxon OX14 4RN

and by Routledge
52 Vanderbilt Avenue, New York, NY 10017

First issued in paperback 2020

Routledge is an imprint of the Taylor & Francis Group, an informa business

British Library Cataloguing-in-Publication Data
A catalogue record for this book is available from the British Library

Library of Congress Cataloging-in-Publication Data
A catalog record for this book has been requested

ISBN 13: 978-0-367-67039-9 (pbk)
ISBN 13: 978-1-138-32240-0 (hbk)

Typeset in Times New Roman by Apex
CoVantage, LLC

Contents

List of figures and tables

Figures

Tables

Acknowledgments

The editor would like to express sincere gratitude to Sung Chull Kim, editor of the *Asian Journal of Peacebuilding* for permission to draw upon the article "Korea's Role for Peacebuilding and Development in Asia," which forms the inspiration for this volume, as well as a significant component of Chapter 5. He is also very grateful to the anonymous reviewers and the Routledge editorial team for their constructive input and support.

This volume grew out of papers presented at the Development Studies Association annual conference "DSA2017: Sustainability Interrogated: Societies, Growth, and Social Justice" at the University of Bradford, September 6–8, 2017. The authors are grateful, therefore, to the funding bodies which supported them in conducting related research and to take part in the conference: Ewha Womans University, JICA-RI, SIPRI, and the Policy-Oriented Research Grant Program through the Korea Foundation.

Notes on contributors

Seon Young Bae graduated with a master's degree in development cooperation from the Graduate School of International Studies at Ewha Womans University. She is currently working as the Communications Officer
in the International Committee of the Red Cross (ICRC) in the South
Korean office.

Brendan Howe is Associate Dean and Professor of International Relations
at the Graduate School of International Studies, Ewha Womans University. He has honorary advisory roles at both the Korean Ministry of Foreign Affairs and the Irish Department of Foreign Affairs and Trade. He
has ongoing research agendas focusing on traditional and nontraditional
security policy-making in East Asia; human security; post-crisis development; democratic governance; and public diplomacy. Major recent works
include *National Security, Statecentricity and Governance in East Asia*
(Springer, 2017); *Peacekeeping and the Asia-Pacific* (Brill, 2016); *Democratic Governance in Northeast Asia* (Springer, 2015); *Post-Conflict
Development in East Asia* (Taylor & Francis, 2014); and *The Protection
and Promotion of Human Security in East Asia* (Palgrave, 2013).

Sachiko Ishikawa is Senior Advisor on Peacebuilding and South–South
Cooperation for the Japan International Cooperation Agency (JICA). She
previously worked for the United Nations High Commissioner for Refugees (UNHCR), the Sasakawa Peace Foundation, and served as Regional
Project Formulation Advisor at both the JICA Thailand Office and JICA
Malaysia Office. Her current research interests are on Japan's peacebuilding in Asia, human security in Southeast Asia, and South–South
cooperation in ASEAN. She received her PhD from Malaysia Science
University in 2013.

Suyoun Jang is a Researcher with the Peace and Development cluster
of studies, Stockholm International Peace Research Institute (SIPRI),

Sweden. She has been seconded to the United Nations Development Programme (UNDP) as Technical Adviser to support the Praia Group on Governance Statistics in Praia, Cape Verde. Her current research is on sustainable development goal (SDG) indicators, the development-humanitarian-peace nexus, and development policies toward conflict-affected fragile states. Recent publications include "Development in Dangerous Places" in the *SIPRI Yearbook 2016*, "Measuring Peacebuilding and Statebuilding in the New SDG Framework" in the *Journal of Peacebuilding and Development* (2016, co-author), and "Development and Security in International Aid to North Korea: Commonalities and Differences among the European Union, the United States and South Korea" in *The Pacific Review* (2017, co-author).

Eun Mee Kim is both Dean of and Professor at the Graduate School of International Studies, Director of the Institute for Development and Human Security, and Director of the Ewha Global Health Institute for Girls at Ewha Womans University. She served as President of the Korea Association of International Development and Cooperation (2011–2012) and was a Member of the Board of Samsung Electronics (2013–2016), the Committee for International Development Cooperation (Prime Minister's Office), and the Policy Advisory Committees of the Ministry of Foreign Affairs and the Ministry of Gender Equality and Family. She received the first research grant to a university in South Korea from the Bill & Melinda Gates Foundation for "Advocacy for Korean Engagement in Global Health and Development" (2013–2016), and for "Korea Global Health Strategy" (2016–2019).

Ako Muto serves as Senior Research Fellow at the JICA Research Institute, involved in research for development, human security, humanitarian crisis, and gender-based violence under conflict-affected situations. The Japan International Cooperation Agency (JICA) is a wing of the Japanese government tasked with providing bilateral Official Development Assistance (ODA) to developing countries. Among other posts, Muto served as Director of Gender Equality Division in its head office and Senior Representative in its Jordan Office before being posted to JICA-RI. She obtained a master's degree in history from the Graduate School of Culture, Keio University, Japan.

Ji Hyun Shin graduated with a master's degree in development cooperation from the Graduate School of International Studies at Ewha Womans University.

1 Introduction

Brendan Howe

Approach and objectives

Peacebuilding, development, and human security are increasingly prominent concepts in diplomatic theory and practice. They pose new challenges to international cooperation and global governance, but also open up space for new actors and initiatives. Northeast and Southeast Asia (hereafter referred to jointly as East Asia) constitute an important region for understanding of both challenges and initiatives. Within this region, Japan and South Korea have been key actors in the promotion of such humanitarian initiatives and policies, significantly to the benefit of regional partner countries, but also in line with the national interests of the Northeast Asian actors. Furthermore, there is potential for collaboration between the two in these fields, even while traditional diplomatic relations between them are strained. Indeed, cooperation in these nontraditional arenas can lead to the improvement of relations between actors.

This research contends that the Republic of Korea (ROK) and Japan can be viewed as middle powers with strategic constraints upon their traditional security policy-making. The concept of middle powers is itself essentially contested, as is the applicability of the term to the two case studies of Japan and South Korea. Thus, this volume will initially identify our operational interpretation of the terminology and will then discuss how it can be applied in both cases (see Chapter 2 "Conceptual framework and intersections"). Essentially, the research will seek to demonstrate what Japan and the ROK have in common in security and foreign policy terms which also distinguishes these two from other regional strategic actors such as the United States (US), China, and Russia. Furthermore, by focusing on two-directional salience, Japan and the ROK will be distinguished from other actors which have contributed significantly to the development and human security of the region such as the US, European Union (EU), and United Nations (UN). Not only are the two Northeast Asian actors incredibly important for the region, but also the region is of great importance for

Japan and South Korea – the other actors mentioned devote a much smaller share of their humanitarian resources to the region.

Both these middle powers find themselves in a hostile operating environment, devoid of multilateral security organizations, with major security challenges emanating from the same sources. In terms of responding to these challenges, both are heavily dependent on close alliances with the US, within which the superpower plays an overwhelmingly dominant role. Both are democracies (a regional rarity) with significant domestic constituency input into their foreign policy output, placing further constraints upon their ability to follow the dictates of *realpolitik*. Both countries, therefore, have felt the need to pursue diplomatic activities raising their international profile or footprint, and to advance national interest through nontraditional security (NTS) and humanitarian channels, including peacebuilding, development, and human security.

Each country has identified several niche areas and pursued initiatives broadly related to the nontraditional and humanitarian lexicon. These include human security and comprehensive security promoted in Tokyo; while Seoul has focused on contribution diplomacy, disaster assessment, coordination, and emergency relief, and institution-building in Southeast Asia. Furthermore, both countries are keen to play expanded roles in the areas of Official Development Assistance (ODA), knowledge transfer and training, peacekeeping operations (PKOs), regional cooperation and integration in Southeast Asia, and countering violent religious extremism. This project assesses the impact of Korean and Japanese NTS policy-making in terms of both beneficial reputational results from the perspective of the actors, and "collateral benefit" for recipients and regional partners.

At the same time, due to historic differences and animosities, Japan and South Korea have achieved little in the field of traditional cooperation despite the shared strategic situation of US alliance and challenges from North Korea and China, and common liberal democratic systems of government. Traditional security issues involve threats to the very existence of a state, and are also caught up with ideas of national sovereignty and identity. Not surprisingly, therefore, under conditions of limited trust and historical overhangs, all states in Northeast Asia have been resistant to any pooling of sovereignty or collective security initiatives, preferring to rely on "self-help" or bilateral military alliances. Yet cooperation in the NTS arena is a very real possibility, with some already documented in PKOs and in the East Asian Summit (EAS). NTS issues are less closely correlated with existential threats to state entities, and therefore cooperation between states becomes more viable, especially when they have a shared interest.

Collaboration in NTS fields can build confidence, lead to a more cooperative wider relationship between actors, and even the evolution of a culture of "yesability" whereby the expectations of parties are those of joint problem-solvers rather than adversaries, even under conditions of animosity (see Fisher, Ury, and Patton 1991). The two countries pooling resources and sharing their know-how in the field would engender a positive image of Japan and Korea as partners; the diplomatic impact of such an image cannot be underestimated, especially in a region where reassurances (from the US) that China would not dominate are presently in short supply. Moreover, consolidating a workable partnership between Japan and Korea is a meaningful confidence-building exercise, which would contribute to improving the bilateral relationship at the people-to-people level. Thus, cooperation on NTS can spill over into the traditional security field, enabling the normalization of relations between Seoul and Tokyo.

This research first, therefore, examines policy arenas for which the niche diplomacy of the two countries is particularly well-suited, assessing the past, present, and future potential of various initiatives. These include a range of related roles in the peacebuilding and humanitarian spectrum revolving around the concepts of human security, human development, and good governance. The secondary purpose of the project is to identify the potential for NTS cooperation between the two countries. Here it is important to note that we will not be addressing concepts of traditional security cooperation in the military sphere between the two countries. Such a study rests beyond the remit of this book. Rather, the focus is on the potential for NTS cooperation between Japan and South Korea not only to benefit vulnerable or fragile populations in regional partner countries, but also to build confidence between the two Northeast Asian actors.

The objectives of this research thus include: (1) identification of the niche diplomatic output of Japan and South Korea in the peacebuilding, development, and human security fields; (2) assessment of the positive contributions these outputs make, not only in terms of the national interest of South Korea and Japan, but also to Southeast Asian partners in and beneficiaries of Seoul and Tokyo's policy-making; (3) evaluation of the promise of synergy between Korean and Japanese humanitarian policy-making; and (4) the potential for cooperation and partnership between these countries and for the wider region. This volume, therefore, assesses the actual and potential NTS and humanitarian niche diplomatic roles played by Japan and South Korea.

Uniqueness of approach

Most works on security policy-making focus on the rational imperative for policymakers to promote national interests, primarily survival of the state in a hostile operating environment, with the secondary consideration of the well-being of the citizens of the state actor. By contrast, most works on humanitarian assistance focus on the normative imperative for those who have the capacity to do so, to do the right thing. This work is unique in that it focuses on the rational imperative and national interests of state-centric actors to carry out peacebuilding, human security, and development cooperation policies. It is in their national interest to do so both in terms of niche diplomacy and security spillover. Furthermore, that it is in the national interest of both Japan and South Korea to carry out humanitarian missions in their near abroad (primarily Southeast Asia), means the potential for greater humanitarian commitment in this region, and increased benefit to the most vulnerable populations.

The second element of uniqueness concerns how the case studies of vulnerable populations are selected. In Chapter 3, Suyoun Jang introduces her analytical framework within which fragility is seen as more than just the measurement of fragile states found in the five most widely used databases. Essentially, her concept of human fragility relates to areas or situations of vulnerability where people face violent death or displacement, and so correlates closely with the human security discourse. Human fragility is identified in the Philippines, and the CLMV countries, Cambodia, Laos, Myanmar, and Vietnam.

The third unique element of the book is its interdisciplinary and holistic nature of the research. Not only do we look at Japanese and Korean perspectives, and incorporate elements of security and development studies, but we also assess policy performance and prescription from the perspectives of Northeast Asian actors and their Southeast Asian partners. While peacebuilding and development have increasingly been addressed in the literature, likewise the relationship between human development and human security, little work has been carried out that addresses all three elements, and none that additionally looks at the spillover between national and human security considerations.

To date, some research has been carried out on South Korean ODA, and on Japanese human security promotion. Likewise, humanitarian challenges in Southeast Asia have received significant coverage. Such work across disciplines and national boundaries, however, has yet to be carried out in a systematic comparative and interactive way, wherein the whole range of NTS niche diplomacy opportunities and challenges confronting Seoul and Tokyo is examined. Likewise, while the role of middle powers is a hot topic both domestically and internationally, the ROK and Japan cases have not been compared. The work on spillover has, almost exclusively, been conducted in the European context, with little analysis of the potential or challenges of the East Asian operating environment.

Chapter overview

Following on from this brief overview of the research project and the volume as a whole, in Chapter 2 Sachiko Ishikawa and Brendan Howe elaborate further the theoretical and conceptual framework and the intersections between different approaches and understandings. This includes first, evaluation of the key concepts of middle powers, niche and new models of diplomacy, and nontraditional security. This is followed by discussion of the intersections between key theoretical and policy perspectives.

Essentially, a middle power is considered to be one that has somewhat middling access to resources, pursues strategies appropriate to middle-powerism, and/or has a modest ability to impact on the external operating environment (Howe 2017, 243–4). Middle powers lack "compulsory power," the military resources to dominate other countries or the economic resources to bribe countries into adopting policies that they would not otherwise pursue. Yet they differ from the small or "system ineffectual" states which have little or no influence. They are, potentially, "system affecting states" which can have a significant impact within a narrower policy area, or in conjunction with others (vom Haua and Hulme 2012, 187–8). To maximize relevance and impact, a degree of selectivity is required, in terms of policy prioritization and/or geographical region. This means the pursuit of "niche diplomacy" which involves concentrating resources in specific areas best able to generate returns worth having, rather than trying to cover the field, allowing them, therefore, to "punch above their weight" (Henrikson 2005, 67).

Ishikawa and Howe note that in recent years there has been increasing policy and academic awareness of the considerable relationship between conflict and development (Mac Ginty and Williams 2016). It has become clear that development issues can escalate and de-escalate conflict. In this context peacebuilding endeavors through development cooperation, especially since UN Secretary-General Boutros Boutros-Ghali's 1992 *Agenda for Peace* (Boutros-Ghali 1992), have been widely implemented across the globe. Furthermore, while security is a concept contested in terms of referent object, the scope of issues covered (the degree of securitization), and within specific issues, the authors point out that NTS agendas have increasingly come to the fore in both academic and policy discourse and are often termed "new security challenges." The characteristics of such challenges include some, or all, of the following: a focus on nonmilitary rather than military threats; transnational rather than national threats; and multilateral or collective rather than self-help security solutions (Acharya 2002; Waever 1995).

Meanwhile, as an emerging multidisciplinary paradigm for understanding global vulnerabilities at the level of individual human beings, human security incorporates methodologies and analysis from several research fields, including strategic and security studies, development studies, human rights, international relations, and the study of international organizations. It exists at the point where these disciplines converge on the concept of protection. The complexity of threats in people's daily lives now involve transnational dimensions and have moved beyond national security, which focused solely on the threat of external military aggressions. Such threats include poverty, unemployment, drugs, terrorism, environmental degradation, and social disintegration, and the concomitant obligations upon those who govern are summed up as a commitment to provide a freedom from fear and a freedom from want (UNDP 1994, 11).

The chapter, therefore, maps the complex network of relationships between the theoretical concepts of peacebuilding, development, and human security, between national and human variants, and between the pursuit of national interest through niche diplomacy and collateral benefit to vulnerable communities in insecure places. It identifies how positive progress and incentives in one area can spill over into others.

In Chapter 3, Suyoun Jang further develops the conceptual framework conventionally used to address "fragile states" as countries that cannot manage economic, environmental, or political shocks and stresses through institutional processes. She conducts a comparison of the five most widely used measurement of fragile states: the Bertelsmann Transformation Index, the Country Indicators for Foreign Policy Fragility Index, the Fragile (formerly Failed) States Index, the Harmonized List of Fragile Situations, and the State Fragility Index, and shows the analytical limitations of the current state-centered approach. The chapter incorporates notions of human security (wherein security is seen as freedom from existential threat to the referent object) and references situations of fragility in which institutions – both state and non-state – have insufficient capacity to resolve disputes, absorb and respond to shocks and stresses, and otherwise create a resilient environment for development.

The concept of human fragility is introduced relating to areas or situations of vulnerability where people face violent death or displacement. The human fragility framework is to complement, not to replace, the current state-centered frameworks by placing subnational variations in the scale of violence, poverty, and marginalized and excluded groups at the center of fragility analysis. From the human fragility perspective, the existence of acute vulnerabilities of people can help define the fragility of society, region, and state in a way to examine why and how such institutions are not successful in reducing vulnerabilities or building resilience. Fragility, therefore, can be analyzed as a "gap" between human fragility and response mechanisms of institutions. Human fragility and such gaps are to be addressed in the context of this book with reference to Southeast Asia, and in particular as they manifest in the Philippines, Cambodia, Laos, Myanmar, and Vietnam.

In Chapter 4 Ako Muto and Sachiko Ishikawa assess Japanese contributions to peacebuilding, development, and human security in East Asia. They note that since the end of the Cold War, the structure of international relations has become more complicated, and that though interstate conflict has been reduced, intrastate conflict, natural disasters, pandemics, and other crises have occurred frequently. Japan has supported the concept of human security with a focus on downside risk and peacebuilding in the context of development cooperation and has expanded the scope of international cooperation to support local communities and vulnerable groups of people. Japan has also given a high priority to Southeast Asia and has been the region's largest aid donor since the late the 1970s (Yanagihara and Emig 1991; Paul 1996, 394). It is stipulated in the Japanese ODA charter that Asia, and in particular the Association of Southeast Asian Nations (ASEAN), "will continue to be a priority region for Japan's ODA" for historical, geographical, political, and economic reasons (MOFA 2003). Thus, for Muto and Ishikawa, human security lies at the heart of Japanese ODA implementation.

They note that Japan has played a very active human security role in Southeast Asia, especially in crisis and disaster response scenarios, as well as upon the global stage. The authors claim that Japan has adopted a tripartite strategy in promoting human security since the middle 1990s involving policy, propaganda, and practice. The policy element will be elaborated through analysis of the Cabinet Decision for the Official Development Assistance (ODA) Charter in 1992, the Medium-Term ODA Policy in 1999 and 2005, the New ODA Charter in 2003, and the Development Cooperation Charter in 2015. In addition to these ODA policies, Japan's creation of peacekeeping law in 1992 provided legal framework for international peacekeeping operations by Japan's Self Defense Forces.

Meanwhile, Japan's efforts in promoting human security in the United Nations arena can be seen as operating at the propaganda level, but also at the level of public and niche diplomacy, especially in terms of network diplomacy. Muto and Ishikawa examine and analyze Japan's contributions in promoting the concept of human security and peacebuilding in the UN arenas such as the Human Security Trust Fund, the Human Security Commission, the Friends of Human Security, and the Peacebuilding Commission. At the practical level, they highlight the case study of Mindanao in the Philippines as a good example of Japan's contribution to peacebuilding, development, and human security in East Asia. They further assess Japan's cooperative actions with regard to human trafficking in ASEAN.

Chapter 5 turns to consideration of South Korean initiatives and contributions. Eun Mee Kim, Brendan Howe, Seon Young Bae, and Ji Hyun Shin point to the extent that recent administrations in Seoul have stressed a commitment to variations on the theme of "principled foreign policy." These have included the "contribution diplomacy" and "Global Korea" agenda pursued by the Lee Myung-bak administration, the aims of which included being "a global actor with broad horizons that engages proactively with the international community in the service of peace and development in the world," a state which "should seek the attributes of a soft, strong power as it builds up its capacities to become a global actor" (Office of the President 2009, 12–13). Subsequently the Park Geun-hye government emphasized the interrelatedness of development cooperation and security and launched its own "middle power diplomacy." Much along these lines is expected of the new liberal administration in Seoul, the diplomatic policy platform of which includes the Global South Policy. This initiative, still under development, is expected to continue and expand the emphasis on the potential of ASEAN countries (and India) as significant development partners for South Korea. Across the board in this region, therefore, Kim and Howe point to there being many opportunities for the ROK to pursue its niche diplomatic diplomacy, much to the benefit of these development partners, but also in the furtherance of Korea's own national diplomatic agenda.

The concluding chapter, Chapter 6, revisits the objectives listed in this introduction in order to assess the extent to which they have been achieved through the intervening chapters. It summarizes the niche diplomatic output of Japan and South Korea in the peacebuilding, development, and human security fields, which were evaluated in Chapters 4 and 5. It further recaps the extent to which these outputs make positive contributions to peacebuilding, development, and human security in the fragile locations and among the vulnerable populations of Southeast Asian partners identified in Chapter 3, while at the same time providing Seoul and Tokyo more bang for their diplomatic bucks. The comparison of policy output and practical impact by Japan and the ROK outlined in Chapters 4 and 5 permits identification of synergy, as well as the potential for cooperation and partnership, in Chapter 6.

Chapter 6 also revisits and develops the concept of spillover as it applies not only to conflict transformation and peacebuilding within fragile locations in Southeast Asia, but also to confidence-building between the Northeast Asian actors. According to David Mitrany (1933, 101), collective governance and "material interdependence" develops its own internal dynamic as states integrate in limited functional, technical, and/or economic areas. This promotes a peaceful and cooperative outlook among actors, not only because everybody is made better off by cooperation, but also because cooperation "spills over" into the high political sphere of security through the establishment of a culture of cooperation rather than conflict.

The chapter further, therefore, identifies how NTS cooperation in the areas of peacebuilding, development, and human security potentially represents just such an area of limited functional, technical, and/or economic integration, and could have a "normalizing" effect on diplomatic relations between Japan and South Korea.

References

Acharya, A. (2002) "Human security: What kind for the Asia Pacific?" in Dickens, D. ed., *The Human Face of Security: Asia-Pacific Perspectives* Australian National University Press, Canberra 5–17.

Boutros-Ghali, B. (1992) *An Agenda for Peace: Preventive Diplomacy, Peacemaking and Peacekeeping* Report of the UN Secretary-General, New York.

Fisher, R., Ury, W., and Patton, B. (1991) *Getting to Yes* Penguin, New York.

Henrikson, A. (2005) "Niche diplomacy in the world public arena: The global 'corners' of Canada and Norway" in Melissen, J. ed., *The New Public Diplomacy: Soft Power in International Relations* Palgrave Macmillan, Basingstoke 67–87.

Howe, B. (2017) "Korea's role for peace-building and development in Asia" *Asian Journal of Peacebuilding* 5(2) 243–66.

Mac Ginty, R. and Williams, A. (2016) *Conflict and Development* 2nd Edition Routledge, Oxford.

Ministry of Foreign Affairs of Japan (MOFA) (2003) *Japan's Official Development Assistance Charter* (www.mofa.go.jp/region/n-america/us/q&a/oda/3.html) Accessed July 12, 2018.

Mitrany, D. (1933) *The Progress of International Government* Yale University Press, New Haven.

Office of the President (2009) *Global Korea: The National Security Strategy of the Republic of Korea* Cheong Wa Dae, Seoul.

Paul, E. (1996) "Japan in Southeast Asia: A geopolitical perspective" *Journal of the Asia Pacific Economy* 1(3) 391–410.

United Nations Development Programme (UNDP) (1994) *Human Development Report: New Dimensions of Human Security* Oxford University Press, New York.

Vom Haua, J. and Hulme, D. (2012) "Beyond the BRICs: Alternative strategies of influence in the global politics of development" *European Journal of Development Research* 24(2) 187–204.

Waever, O. (1995) "Securitization and desecuritization" in Lipschutz, R. D. ed., *On Security* Columbia University Press, New York 46–86.

Yanagihara, T. and Emig, A. (1991) "An overview of Japan's foreign aid" in Islam, S. ed., *Yen for Development: Japanese Foreign Aid and the Politics of Burden-Sharing* Council on Foreign Relations Press, New York 37–69.

2 Conceptual framework and intersections

Peacebuilding, development, and human security

Sachiko Ishikawa and Brendan Howe

Middle powers and niche diplomacy

The notions of what it is to be a middle power and how the power of aspirants is to be measured are challenging to define. Ashley Tellis et al. note that most notions of power boil down to references to "allocation of resources," "ability to use these resources," and the "strategic character" of power, meaning its use not only against inertia, but also opposing wills. "This tripartite approach to power can be restated using a simple taxonomy that describes power as 'resources,' as 'strategies,' and as 'outcomes'" (Tellis et al. 2000, 13–14). Thus, a middle power is one that has somewhat middling access to resources, pursues strategies appropriate to middle-powerism, and/or has a modest ability to impact on the external operating environment (Howe 2017a, 243–4).

South Korea and Japan certainly do not fall in the middle of the pack of global power rankings. South Korea ranks in the global top ten for military expenditure at US$36 billion/annum, and has the world's seventh largest army at 630,000 active personnel with an additional 2,900,000 personnel in the reserves, and the sixth largest air force, with up-to-date power-projection capabilities (MND 2015). The Korean economy currently ranks just outside the global top ten national economies by GDP (nominal) at almost US$1.5 trillion and is predicted to move up from 11th in 2016 to 7th by 2030 (Statistics Times 2016). It is also a member of both the Organisation for Economic Co-operation and Development (OECD) "rich man's club" of nations, and the Group of Twenty (G20).

Japan, historically, has certainly been more of a great power, defeating one future superpower at the start of the 20th century (Russia), and challenging two hegemons for regional and potentially global dominance (the United Kingdom and the US). After recovering from defeat in World War II (WWII), for much of the intervening period Japan held on to second spot in global economic rankings, only being overtaken by China in the

21st century. Japan is ranked two places above the ROK in terms of military expenditure at 8th in the world and maintains one of the most modern militaries (SIPRI 2017). Yet internal and external constraints limit the extent to which either country can wield this latent traditional power, based on resources in terms of both strategies and outcomes in the contemporary operating environment.

Despite the country achieving significant economic development since being defeated in WWII, Soeya (2005) explicitly categorizes Japan as a middle power, due to its unidimensional influence on world affairs. Kent Calder (1988, 518–28), the originator of the "reactive state" hypothesis, downgrades Japan even further than middle power status, seeing the country as occupying the unique position of having the power potential of a mid-range European state, yet the political leverage of much smaller and weaker reactive states. Calder claims that the fragmented character of state authority in Japan makes decisive action more difficult than in countries with strong chief executives, such as the US, thereby explaining Japanese passivity in international affairs when activism would have been both possible and beneficial for Japan.

Such has been the impact of Calder's hypothesis that the dominant view of Japan's international behavior is one where Japan is portrayed as passive, risk-avoiding, and ineffective in conducting foreign policy (Hirata 1998, 1). Hence, Calder (2005) has more recently claimed that his major contentions have weathered the test of time, noting that Japan has not, despite a huge economy, emerged as an effective "rule-maker" in international affairs. It has even been claimed that "Japan has a psychological disadvantage in dealing with the United States" which relegates it to the status of junior partner or pupil (Taira 1991, 161–2).

Meanwhile, in South Korea, relative lack of resources compared with those of strategic competitors limits the country's role options. For Ray Cline (1977, 34), Perceived Power (Pp) is a function of Critical Mass (C = Population + Territory), Economic Capability (E), Military Capability (M), Strategic Purpose (S), and Will to Pursue National Strategy (W), where $Pp = (C+E+M) \times (S+W)$. Strategic Purpose and Will more properly fit into the strategies box, with the potential to impact on the outcomes category. The problems for the ROK stem from C (Population + Territory) in terms of resources, combined with character of the strategic operating environment within which the country finds itself (Howe 2017b, 5).

These are the considerations which, despite significant M and E resources, have led the ROK to be perceived, both internally and externally, as something of a "shrimp among whales." Kalinowski and Cho (2012, 244) point to still further limitations on South Korea's policy options noting that due to geopolitical constraints the ROK is unable to perform the traditional neutral or brokering role of middle powers.

This volume contends, however, that despite strategic obstacles to effective independent policy-making and international influence in the realm of traditional security, nevertheless, both Japan and South Korea have been proactive rather than reactive in the nontraditional security arena of peacebuilding, development, and human security. Furthermore, the evolution of international society has opened additional avenues for the pursuit of related niche diplomatic activities. The end of the Cold War has empowered the activism of a new generation of middle powers. Unlike "old" models of diplomacy, "new" diplomatic initiatives can be wielded by a variety of state and non-state actors, even if they lack traditional power resources. The rapidly shifting nature of peacebuilding and development cooperation in the 21st century presents middle powers with a "noble opportunity" to do something that is both normatively right and beneficial to others, while also in the national interest (Lee 2014, 2–3).

At the same time, the complexities of the relationships between peacebuilding, development, and human security, and the increasing sophistication of the theoretical modeling of these relationships (in Figure 2.1), reflect both greater potential for positive contributions from these external actors and challenges to them. Due to spillovers between the paradigms in practice, it becomes possible to contribute to all by aiding one. Yet exogenous interventions are likely to fail, or even be counter-productive, if not directed through the empowerment of endogenous actors and the individuals and groups most requiring change in their circumstances. The next section presents an overview of the spillover between levels of insecurity.

Security and insecurity

In recent years there has been increasing policy and academic awareness of the considerable relationship between conflict and development (Mac Ginty and Williams 2016). It has become clear that development issues can escalate and de-escalate conflict. Furthermore, policy and governance conceptual evolution in the post–Cold War era required the international society to widen its scope from peacekeeping, to peacemaking and peacebuilding, in order to cope with increasing intrastate conflicts, which afterward demand reconstruction and development works. In this context, peacebuilding endeavors through development cooperation, especially since UN Secretary-General Boutros Boutros-Ghali's 1992 *Agenda for Peace* (Boutros-Ghali 1992), have been widely implemented across the globe.

Despite the decline of interstate wars, militarized international disputes (MIDs) continue, and intrastate conflicts and their legacies threaten directly the lives and livelihoods of the most vulnerable. Such threats extend beyond the official cessation of hostilities through conflictual legacies such as contamination by the explosive remnants of war (ERW), socioeconomic disruption, governance failure, and environmental degradation. Conflictual operating environments also pose indirect threats to the human security of the most vulnerable. These include the securitization of governance, the normalization of state violence, contamination of the environment, and the diversion of resources to national defense projects.

Hence, security itself has become an essentially contested concept. Security is contested in terms of referent object, the scope of issues covered, the degree of securitization, and indeed within specific issues. Nontraditional security (NTS) agendas have increasingly come to the fore in both academic and policy discourse and are often termed "new security challenges." The characteristics of such challenges include some, or all, of the following: a focus on nonmilitary rather than military threats; transnational rather than national threats; and multilateral or collective rather than self-help security solutions (Acharya 2002; Wæver 1995). Yet, although they are distinct in terms of focus and (when looking at elements of human security) referent objects, there remains a close relationship between traditional and nontraditional security approaches. All forms of security address the notion of a referent object free from threats to its continued existence. Likewise, insecurity means that the referent object is not able to enjoy such freedom from threat. Vulnerabilities relate to the likelihood that the referent object(s) will be exposed to existential threats.

Furthermore, national insecurity (wherein those acting in its name perceive there to be existential threats to the state) may lead to human insecurity (existential threats to the lives of individuals) along various paths. It can divert resources from human development, which in turn focuses on "human flourishing" or improving the lives of people rather than the richness of the national economy (UNDP 2015). It can drain energy (Suh 2013, 4). It can create a permissive political circumstance where national security is privileged at all costs (Unger 2012). It is also likely to produce and perpetuate an operating environment within which the exceptional use of internal as well as external violence by the state becomes a permanent feature of the state (Suh 2013, 5). The human costs of modern conflicts, whether interstate or intrastate, are borne, primarily, by the most vulnerable sections of society (Tirman 2015). Civilians can be directly targeted, used as human shields, or become the victims of "collateral damage" during conflicts.

The legacies of conflicts can impact on the human security of the most vulnerable for years, decades, or even generations to come (Watson 2004, 4). Postbellum threats to both life and well-being include the breakdown of law and order, the spread of disease due to refugee camp overcrowding, poor nutrition, infrastructure collapse, scarcity of medical supplies (although ironically often a proliferation of illicit drugs), continued criminal attacks on civilian populations, unemployment, displacement, homelessness, disrupted economic activity, stagflation, and perhaps most directly, ERW contamination (GICHD 2007; UNDP 2016). Negative effects include physical harm, amputation and death, psychological trauma, food insecurity, infrastructure limitations, and increased rebuilding costs.

The relationship between different conceptualizations of security has been addressed through the concept of security spillover, which was first introduced by functionalists such as the pioneering David Mitrany (1933), and further developed by neo-functionalists like Ernst Haas (1958, 1964). In its traditional formulation, cooperation between states in one field would spill over into cooperation in other fields. It has further been embraced by English School rationalists, who look to the "civilizing" effect that cooperation within international institutions can have on policymakers, and social constructivists, who look at the mutually constitutive nature of agents and rules in international society. This chapter will also, however, look at how human (in)security can spill over into its national variant and vice versa, as well as how underdevelopment can spill over into insecurity at both the national and human level.

Thus, conflict, development, security (in all its manifestations), and the complex network of relationships between these concepts, all need to be considered when attempting to build peace. The next three sections consider the evolution of the theoretical framework of peacebuilding as it has adapted to the demands of development and human security. The first addresses the growing awareness of the necessity of attending to developmental needs in order to secure a lasting and comprehensive peace. This is followed by a section on the operationalization of peacebuilding within the context of a human security perspective, and finally a section considering the relationship between human security and development.

Building peace with development

Before WWII, peace was commonly understood as the absence of hostilities and considered to be synonymous with national security (Mogami 2006, 90–8). As a result of the tremendous number of casualties and development of nuclear weapons during this global conflict, preventing the recurrence of war has increasingly come to occupy a central position in peace research (Wallensteen 2007, 5). During the post-war period, there have been three significant phases in the field of peace and conflict studies, reflecting increased engagement of peace research with the development agenda.

The first phase was the evolution of the notion of positive peace – as distinguished from that of negative peace – by Johan Galtung in the late 1960s. This was followed by Edward Azar's protracted social conflict or PSC theory in the 1980s. Azar, together with John Burton (1987, 1990), Herbert Kelman (1992, 1996), and other scholars, eventually developed the problem-solving approach, which was the combination of peace mediation and development work. The third phase was the concept of "peacebuilding from below," presented by John Paul Lederach in the late 1990s. While Azar's PSC theory described development in the context of peacebuilding as third parties' external assistance, Lederach's concept of "peacebuilding from below" articulated that local people should be the main actors of peacebuilding while recognizing third parties as partners of local initiatives.

Positive peace

The concept of positive peace broadened the potential of human life by incorporating the concept of development. During the period stretching from the 1950s to the 1960s, there were two significant schools of thought on how peace research should be defined, resulting in a struggle between European structuralists and North American pragmatists (Ramsbotham, Woodhouse, and Miall 2005, 42). While Kenneth Boulding (1961, 1962) and his colleagues from the University of Michigan concentrated on the issue of preventing war – and nuclear war in particular – Johan Galtung reframed the debate toward the concepts of positive and negative peace. This influenced the way knowledge and skills for achieving peace developed (Jeong 2000, 27). Galtung's contribution to redefining the concept of peace was rooted in his detailed observation of violence. He categorized violence into three different types: direct violence, structural violence, and cultural violence. While direct violence was not a new concept, the structural and cultural types allowed different perspectives on conflict and peace.

Structural violence is characterized by uneven life opportunities, inequitable distribution of resources, and unequal decision-making power, which are caused by social ills such as poverty, hunger, and denial of educational opportunities (Jeong 2000, 20). Due to its indirect and insidious nature, structural violence often works slowly in eroding human values. Galtung argued that structural violence is typically built into the very structure of society and cultural institutions (Galtung 1969, 14). Cultural violence involves hatred, fear, and suspicion, which are most often caused by the symbolic sphere of our existence, such as religion, ideology, art, and so forth (Galtung 1990, 291).

Based on his categorizations of violence, Galtung defined negative peace as the absence of direct violence, while positive peace guaranteed life-sustaining human conditions by overcoming cultural and structural violence (Jeong 2000, 23). Positive peace advocates social change toward realizing human potential and justice by providing equal opportunities and equitable distribution of resources. In this context, development plays a role in building positive peace, which provides a foundation for the significant role of development in peacebuilding.

At this level, we can see the mutually constitutive nature of development and security. International policy debate and action have highlighted the importance of security in the context of global poverty reduction. In particular, *The Millennium Development Goals Report 2008* (UN 2008) addressed the issue of "conflict" as an important causal factor in the generation and perpetuation of poverty through mechanisms such as displacement (internally displaced persons and cross-border refugee flows) and food security (scarcity and price inflation). Therefore, not only is there a direct causal relationship between insecurity and poverty but the solution to poverty must also encompass the means to address security problems.

Conflict creates specific constraints for the formulation of good governance programs in general – and poverty reduction strategies in particular. In addition to creating specific types and manifestations of poverty, conflict also affects wider structures and institutions (Musoni 2003, 3). At the same time, however, the literature in this section draws attention to underdevelopment or unequal development as a conflict driver. Thus, a solution for conflict must also encompass means to address inequalities and lack of distributive justice. This element of the relationship has been developed further in the works of Edward Azar and John Burton, and those of their followers.

Protracted social conflict theory

Edward Azar's protracted social conflict theory explicitly placed importance on development as a means of achieving positive peace. Azar's contributions to conflict and peace studies were his trailblazing efforts in linking conflict analysis and resolution with economic, political, and social development (Fisher 1997, 97). Although Azar's early academic career was centered on quantitative international relations, his focus subsequently shifted to ethnic conflict in the third world (Azar 1983). He was then convinced that it was necessary to shift the focus in international relations from strategic interaction, deterrence, crisis management, and the containment of violence between the superpowers, to an acknowledgement that two-thirds of the world's states were small, poorly defined, destitute, and highly vulnerable to both ethnic cleavages and negative international influences (Azar 1983, 81–9).

Based on this conceptual transformation, Azar developed a model known as protracted social conflict (PSC) theory. He defined the concept of PSC as hostile interactions between identity groups that continue over a long period of time with sporadic outbreaks of open warfare fluctuating in frequency and intensity (Azar 1990, 6). Azar gradually operationalized his PSC theory by serving as a third-party facilitator in problem-solving workshops for various conflicts. The emphasis given to issues such as security, identity, and recognition in problem-solving workshops led to a realization of the importance of basic human needs. Azar then reached the conclusion that it was necessary to explore the relationship between conflict and development factors, including structural inequality, resource maldistribution, population dynamics, ineffective development projects, and ethnic struggles within the postcolonial context (Azar 1983, 96). In particular, he pointed out that the reduction of underdevelopment could be a requirement of reducing overt conflict (Azar 1990, 155).

Based on Azar's PSC theory, John Burton (1987) presented the concept of deep-rooted conflict, which in turn was based on issues of cultural identity, denial of recognition and participation of minorities, and an absence of security and other essentials that were nonnegotiable. Burton and others then developed "needs theory" through a problem-solving approach by attempting to identify basic human needs, such as identity, security, freedom, participation, and justice, and then searching for mechanisms that would ensure they were not denied (Burton 1990). While traditional approaches to negotiation and mediation deal with the interests of negotiating parties, the problem-solving approach focuses on nonnegotiable needs of all parties and tries to find ways of satisfying those needs in order to solve the conflict.

Azar eventually also adopted and used the problem-solving approach within a four-step process for the management of PSCs. These steps are: (1) tracking the conflict, (2) facilitating breakthroughs through workshops, (3) promoting structural development within the society, and (4) adopting development diplomacy to alleviate external barriers to resolution (Fisher 1997, 88). Azar's PSC theory gave legitimacy to development playing a role in peacebuilding.

There are three significant implications of addressing PSCs in relation to development. First, PSC theory identifies the problems of structural inequality and need deprivation as the core causes for perpetuating a conflict, while traditional approaches simply focus on the symptoms of violence. Second, PSC theory suggests dual approaches to solve conflicts, such as short-term interventions through problem-solving workshops and also long-term efforts to transform conflict situations, particularly with development diplomacy (Azar 1990, 96–104). Development diplomacy is designed to promote structural improvements by addressing needs and communal imbalances. Third, PSC theory (and John Burton's problem-solving workshops) suggests that third parties should deal with identity groups through face-to-face interactions in order to identify both needs and means to satisfy them.

This method complements development diplomacy to consolidate the transformation of the conflict. However, it should be noted that, at this stage, local communities and people are still regarded as beneficiaries of largesse in the development context. A further theoretical and operational leap was required before people were placed center-stage in the processes of overcoming conflict-related challenges through engagement with needs.

Peacebuilding from below

The third phase in the evolution of peace and conflict studies was the idea of empowering people and civil society. This eventually evolved into the concept of "peacebuilding from below," introduced by John Paul Lederach. Prior to discussing the work of Lederach, it is necessary to examine track-two diplomacy and multi-track diplomacy as developed by, among others, Adam Curle (1971), paving the way for the concept of "peacebuilding from below." Curle built up the process of peacemaking through a progression of changing relationships between antagonists so that they might be brought to the point where development could occur (Curle 1971). He elaborated that development would involve the restructuring of relationships so that the conflict that had previously rendered such relationships unpeaceful could be eliminated and replaced by collaboration that would prevent conflict from recurring (Curle 1971).

Curle (1986) proposed a soft-track mediation approach, which was based on the human development concept as well as humanistic psychology. In the late 1980s Curle, Montville, McDonald, and Bendahmane further developed Curle's soft-track mediation approach into a strategy referred to as track-two diplomacy, which would be complementary to traditional, state-to-state diplomacy and could assist in de-escalating conflicts and improving relations between antagonistic parties (Montville 1987). McDonald and Diamond further proposed a "multi-track diplomacy," which suggested the process of defining and describing the whole picture of newly emerged conflicts (Diamond and McDonald 1996, 4). This approach consists of nine tracks in a conceptual and practical framework involving private citizens, nongovernmental movements, and business sectors as actors of peacebuilding (Diamond and McDonald 1996, 4–5).

Along with the idea of multi-track diplomacy, there were shifts in thinking which moved the emphasis in conflict resolution work from an outsider-neutral approach toward a partnership with local actors, and it was this relationship that was one of the key characteristics of peacebuilding from below (Ramsbotham, Woodhouse, and Miall 2005). The task is to empower people of goodwill in conflict-affected communities to rebuild democratic institutions and help in the development of local peacemakers (Woodhouse 2010, 6).

While Lederach developed his concept from Curle's soft-track mediation approach, as well as the subsequent track-two diplomacy and multi-track diplomacy concepts, his idea of "peacebuilding from below" articulated a clear goal for peace, which was reconciliation (Lederach 1999). His peace-building concept departed from merely post-conflict reconstruction, suggested previously in *An Agenda for Peace* (Boutros-Ghali 1992). Indeed, Lederach contends that peacebuilding is much more than post-accord reconstruction. Peacebuilding is understood as a comprehensive concept that encompasses, generates, and sustains the full array of processes, approaches, and stages needed to transform conflict toward more sustainable, peaceful relationships. The term "peacebuilding from below" thus involves a wide range of activities and functions that both precede and follow formal peace accords. Peace is a dynamic social construct, which requires a process akin to that of constructing a building: collecting investments and materials, developing the architectural design, coordinating labor, laying the foundations, and overseeing detailed finishing work, as well as ensuring continuous maintenance (Lederach 1997, 20).

In order to explain the comprehensive approach to peacebuilding, Lederach presented two essential frameworks: the structure of conflict-affected societies and the integrated framework of peacebuilding. The first framework presents three types of actors (top leadership, middle-range actors, and grassroots actors) and related approaches to peacebuilding (top-down approach, middle-out approach, and bottom-up approach). In particular, the bottom-up approach of grassroots actors was essential for the concept of "peacebuilding from below." Lederach argued that the greatest resources for sustaining peace in the long-term were always rooted in the local people and their cultures. He thus suggested that the international community should see people living in the setting as resources, not recipients. In other words, citizen-based peacemaking must be seen as instrumental and integral, not peripheral, to sustaining change (Lederach 1997, 94).

In fact, Lederach's concept of empowerment of local society closely parallels the evolution of the international discourse on human security further developed below. He articulated that the international community should adopt a new mindset and move beyond a simple prescription of answers and modalities for dealing with conflict that come from outside the setting and focus at least as much attention on discovering and empowering the resources, modalities, and mechanisms for building peace that exist within the context (Lederach 1997, 95). Lederach's model of a bottom-up approach provides a convincing means for setting the medium-term perspective of institution and nation building within the longer-term goal of human security-oriented peacebuilding and reconciliation (Ramsbotham, Woodhouse, and Miall 2005, 226).

In Lederach's second framework, an integrated framework for peacebuilding, transformation was the key idea. The concept of transformation poses a question of how protagonists get from crisis to desired change and provides a paradigm shift of peacebuilding from merely a post-conflict process manipulated by elite groups, to participatory and people-centric processes throughout the whole time frame of activities, including in-conflict settings (Lederach 1997, 79–85). He argues that transformation requires input from four other factors: root causes, crisis management, prevention, and vision. He also suggests that conflict transformation refers to change that can be understood in two fundamental ways – descriptively and prescriptively – across four dimensions, which are personal, relational, structural, and cultural. In the descriptive modality, transformation refers to the empirical impact of conflict, while at a prescriptive level, transformation refers to the goals that are anticipated by a people and a society in conflict (Lederach 1997, 82).

Lederach's concept of peacebuilding from below is recognized as a revision in thinking of the traditional notion of post-conflict peacebuilding (Ramsbotham, Woodhouse, and Miall 2005). He suggested that one-dimensional interventions by external actors would be unlikely to produce comprehensive or lasting resolutions. Post-conflict peacebuilding needs to be underpinned by structures and long-term development frameworks that will erode cultures of violence and sustain peace processes on the ground. Local actors with local wisdom are to enhance sustainable citizen-based peacebuilding initiatives and to open up participatory public political spaces in order to allow institutions of civil society to flourish (Ramsbotham, Woodhouse, and Miall 2005, 215–6).

As examined in this section, since the 1960s, there has been a gradual evolution in the study of conflict and prescriptions for the building of peace to reflect an ever-greater awareness of the relationship or spillover between the concepts of conflict, development, and peacebuilding. As fields, peacebuilding and development have also evolved in both theory and practice, most recently reflecting the impact of the newly prominent human security paradigm.

Building peace while reflecting human security

Figure 2.1 presents a chronological overview of the three stages of the peacebuilding literature discussed in the previous section, reflecting its engagement with human security concepts and its operationalization through actors and activities.

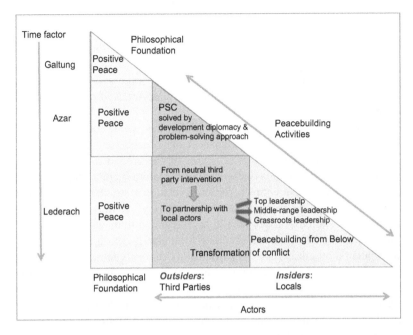

Figure 2.1 Chronology of peacebuilding theories

As shown in the figure, Galtung's positive peace has remained the constant solid philosophical foundation until today. Azar's PSC theory and Lederach's theory on the transformation of conflict – particularly the concept of "peacebuilding from below" – are aligned with the concept of positive peace. In this figure, positive peace represents a guarantee of positive human conditions by overcoming the remaining cultural and structural violence. Conditions for positive peace can be built either after the absence of direct violence has already been achieved (normally with a cease-fire agreement or a peace agreement) or as part of a process to eradicate direct violence (normally in-conflict). Galtung's concept of positive peace, together with his model of conflict, therefore, set the foundation for peacebuilding from a human security perspective.

Azar and Burton's analyses of PSC and deep-rooted conflict have clarified a new dimension concerning conflicts in the post–Cold War era. These conflicts required attention to cultural difference, ethnicity, language, identity, economic disparities, and so forth in order to identify the needs of protagonists. In this sense, development has become an important element for conflict resolution, a point that PSC theory viewed as the foundation for the process of peacebuilding (Fisher 1993). As shown in Figure 2.1, however, it should be stressed that PSC theory focuses more on third-party interventions than proactive activities initiated by protagonists or local actors. Fisher (1993, 247–66) subsequently defined peacebuilding at this stage as those developmental and interactive activities, often facilitated by a third party, that are directed toward meeting basic needs, de-escalating hostility, and improving the relationship of parties engaged in protracted social conflict.

Finally, in the evolution of peacebuilding theory, the focus has shifted to local actors, with Lederach's concept of "peacebuilding from below." Lederach documented a number of cases on the ground where traditional third-party interventions alone were not effective in resolving conflicts without paying close attention to personal, relational, structural, and cultural dimensions, both descriptively and prescriptively. He thus proposed conflict transformation as a key idea in his integrated framework, which provides a paradigm shift of peacebuilding from merely a post-conflict process manipulated by elite groups to participatory and people-centric processes through the whole extended process of activities, including in-conflict settings. Lederach then presented the model of "Actors and Approaches to Peacebuilding" in order to articulate how local participatory process can be implemented. In these respects, Lederach's transformation theory further reflects the concept of human security.

With regard to the third-party interventions in Lederach's model, the paradigm of peacebuilding has shifted to insider endeavors from outsider elite interventions or conscientious assistance. Although Lederach acknowledged the "do no harm" concept, presented by Mary Anderson (1999), as a minimum requirement for third-party involvement in peacebuilding, his "peacebuilding from below" further elaborated that outsiders could be partners of local actors (Lederach 1997). Third parties can assist local actors in the aforementioned three levels of establishing cultural-based peace constituencies, and also in sustaining and consolidating them to transform a conflict into a more peaceful relationship among local actors.

Thus, the evolution of the peacebuilding discourse has increasingly come to reflect the central tenets of human security: the necessity of providing conditions under which individuals and vulnerable groups can live their lives free from fear, free from want, and in dignity. Furthermore, the discourse increasingly recognizes, as does the human security paradigm, that these aspirations cannot simply be provided for individuals and groups by exogenous "benefactors," but rather that these communities must be empowered to achieve such goals for themselves. As shown above, the conceptual transformation in peacebuilding pays special attention to the role of development and human security. In addition to this, there are a number of conditions that must be met in order to incorporate the concept of human security into peacebuilding. These include:

1 adopting the concept of positive peace as the foundation for guaranteeing positive human conditions by overcoming cultural and structural violence;
2 recognizing protracted social conflicts as the main targets to be addressed;
3 recognizing transformation of conflict up to the level of reconciliation as a goal for peacebuilding, for which local populations are regarded not as beneficiaries but as the main actors;
4 understanding, in connection with conflict transformation, that peacebuilding is not merely post-conflict reconstruction but continuous endeavors in pre- and in-conflict situations;
5 restating that development aspects can play an important part in transformation of protracted social conflicts toward more peaceful relationships among protagonists; and
6 emphasizing that third parties' involvement in peacebuilding should be as partners of local actors for assisting local efforts in their cultural settings.

Developmental perspectives of human security

In the post–Cold War era, two significant streams of thought have emerged in the field of development studies. First, as the number of intrastate conflicts burgeoned in 1990s, Paul Collier's "greed and grievance" theory (Collier 2000) became influential in explaining the relationship between poverty and conflict. Although fiercely debated and critiqued, the concept of "greed and grievance" posed a fundamental challenge to the traditional development discourse. In short, the theory argues, within the framework of contemporary civil wars, greed trumps grievance as a motivation of war and that international responses need to be reconsidered in that light (Gorman 2011). A number of other scholars have, however, presented a different view, attesting that conflicts are caused by a combination of factors (Mac Ginty and Williams 2016; Homer-Dixon 1994; Sen 2006). So far, the academic debate on "greed and grievance" theory has, at least, reached a consensus that both greed and grievance are responsible for the outbreak of intrastate conflict (Ballentine and Nitzchke 2003).

The question of neoliberal preponderance or even hegemony was the second challenging theoretical perspective to be addressed in relation to post-conflict international development aid and, due to its interstate nature, it provoked lengthy debates not only in development studies but also among

scholars of international relations. The collapse of the Soviet Union signi-
fied the demise of alternative models of economies and, thus, pursuing a
market economy and democratization became the only choice for development and the condition for development aid. When the notion of neoliberalism was adopted by developed Western countries as a policy prescription
and a norm for their peacebuilding activities, it constituted liberal peace
theory focusing on constitutional democracy, human rights, a free and glo-
balized market, and neoliberal development (Richmond 2006). Ultimately
the liberal peace hypothesis came under immense criticism particularly with
regard to its inability to address poverty and social exclusion (Lal 1998;
Dorn 1998; Harvey 2005).

A number of contributors have analyzed the shortcomings of the liberal
peace discourse. Among others, Newman, Paris, and Richmond (2009)
have pointed out two major defects. First, Western democracies are not
necessarily suitable for volatile societies that do not enjoy stable institutions. Second, international peacebuilding is not really liberal when
it tends to mediate between local powerbrokers and ignores grassroots
community actors, who are potentially more inclusive and moderate (Tadjbakhsh 2010).

Richmond has, instead, presented an emancipatory model, which is more
critical of liberal peace (Richmond 2006). This emancipatory model is concerned with a much closer relationship of custodianship and consent with
local ownership, and tends to be very critical of coerciveness, conditionality,
and dependency. This can be seen as correlating closely with the bottom-
up approach to peacebuilding outlined previously, while also emphasizing
needs-based activities and a stronger concern for social welfare and justice,
as reflected in broad interpretations of human security. Such a peace equates
to civil peace, and generally is not state-led, but rather is shaped by private
actors and social movements. His emancipatory model has been influential
due to the fact that it offered a solid base for academic debate among scholars in development studies as well as international relations. However, the
most significant contribution of the emancipatory model has been to draw
the perspective of human security into the debate on liberal peace as a con-
nector between people and the state (Richmond 2007; Begby and Burgess
2009; Peterson 2009).

According to Richmond (2007), there are two key versions of human
security: the institutional approach and the emancipatory approach. The
institutional approach corresponds to the "top-down" approach and depends
on the security of strong state structures and international intervention driven
by hegemonic states that establish the necessary institutions to provide for
very basic forms of human security. By contrast, the emancipatory approach
is a "bottom-up" one where individuals are empowered to negotiate and

develop forms of human security that fit their political, economic, and social needs, while also providing them with the tools necessary to do so.

Institutional human security can itself be seen as a tool for external actors to justify their post-conflict intervention as being carried out in order to protect people's physical and economic security. Due to a number of failure cases of such liberal peacebuilding, questions have been posed as to what should be done in order to create self-sustainable peace. Most scholars have, however, been able to reach a key point of agreement on the vital role that non-state actors play in peacebuilding and indeed that global governance would not possible without their cooperation. In conclusion, Richmond argues that human-security-oriented peacebuilding activities must move beyond the confines of institutional approaches into a terrain where emancipation is achieved – and concurrent legitimacy is gained – rather than relying on conditionality, occasional coercion, cooption, and ignoring crucial factors such as welfare, employment, culture, and the rights of the most marginalized groups (Richmond 2007).

Rectifying economic disparities and achieving the well-being of vulnerable individuals and groups has become the central agenda for development studies. In particular, poverty alleviation has been a core development issue among the international aid community since the 1980s. An embryonic conceptualization of human security can be observed in some of the approaches put forward during the Cold War period, such as the theories of endogenous development, self-reliance, and empowerment. These theories, however, lack the perspective of intrastate conflict or peacebuilding. During the post–Cold War era, while the "greed and grievance" theory dealt with the cause of conflict in the political-economy context, the failure of the "liberal peace" discourse led to questions over the intervention of external actors in peacebuilding. Subsequently, the emancipatory approach of human security was put forward within the "liberal peace" framework.

Development and human security can, likewise, be viewed as mutually supporting or even mutually constitutive. A peaceful environment frees individuals and governments to move from a focus on mere survival to a position where they can consider improvement of their situations. Likewise, as a society develops, it is able to afford more doctors, hospitals, welfare networks, internal security operations, schools, and de-mining operations. Conversely, conflict retards development, and underdevelopment can lead to conflict, as detailed above.

Crucially, development of the wrong sort can negatively impact on the human security of the most vulnerable. Development mega-projects such as hydroelectric dams require the relocation of vulnerable groups, often increasing their insecurity. Making a country "land-linked" rather than "land-locked" through transportation infrastructure development can lead to an increase in traffic accidents, human and drug trafficking, and the spread of disease. The development of plantations and industrial farming can displace people from the land. "Modernization" in the form of industrialization can endanger the human security of the most vulnerable through unsafe working conditions, poisoning the air they breathe, the water they drink, and the food they eat.

This section has examined the intertwined relationship between development and conflict through an analysis of the debates on liberal peace theory, which in turn involved human security. The chapter has, thus far, introduced peacebuilding, development, and human security as deeply interrelated paradigms. The next section further models and clarifies the integral and holistic approach taken in this volume to addressing the challenges associated with the approaches.

Mapping intersections among peacebuilding, development, and human security

Based on the discussions so far on peacebuilding, human security, and development, this section tries to integrate the different threads of discussion and map the intertwined concepts of peacebuilding, development, and human security. For this purpose, there are two core questions to be answered. The first concerns whether the emancipatory approach of human security is synonymous with "peacebuilding from below." If not, what are the common and divergent points between the two concepts? Second, if the emancipatory approach of human security and the concept of "peacebuilding from below" are roughly synonymous or are, at least, connected with the notion of a "bottom-up" approach, what is the best strategy to follow in order to realize a self-sustainable peace through the "bottom-up" concept?

In order to deal with the first question, the different natures and backgrounds of the two concepts need to be clarified. A basic comparison between the two concepts is shown in Table 2.1. The two concepts share two important considerations: "for what?" (objectives) and "for whom?" (beneficiaries). The common objective of the two concepts is to achieve self-sustainable peace for local people and communities.

There are, however, two significant differences between the two concepts. The first concerns the matters of when and who (actors). The emancipatory approach of human security is a by-product of and development from liberal peace. The concept thus focuses on development issues, reconstruction, and governance, in particular during a post-conflict period. As a characteristic of development studies, the emancipatory approach of human security still comes from the viewpoint of third parties, which must be sensitive enough about local culture and traditions to put themselves in a position to help emancipate local actors (Tadjbakhsh 2010, 129). On the other

Table 2.1 Comparison between the emancipatory approach of human security and peacebuilding from below

	Emancipatory approach of HS (from an outsider perspective)	*Peacebuilding from below (from and insider perspective)*
Background (field of study)	Development Studies & International Relations (IR)	Peace Studies
Why (aim)?	For self-sustainable peace	For self-sustainable peace
What needs to be dealt with?	Development issues (e.g. reconstruction, governance)	Conflict transformation aimed at reconciliation (development issues can be included)
When?	Post-conflict	Pre-, in-, and post-conflict
Where?	Conflict-affected areas and countries	Conflict-affected areas and countries
Who (actors)?	Third parties (both international and local)	Locals (third parties have a secondary role)
For whom (beneficiaries)?	Local people and communities	Local people and communities
Against what?	Liberal peacebuilding (Western hegemonic values)	Injustice inside the country (pre- and in-conflict) Liberal peacebuilding (post-conflict)
How (method)?	Bottom-up approach by empowering locals	Bottom-up approach by self-empowerment of locals

hand, "peacebuilding from below" covers broader issues under the concept of conflict transformation during all conflict stages including that of in-conflict. In this concept, the main actors are local people and communities, and from this perspective, human security should focus on self-empowerment of people and communities while third parties play only a secondary role in assisting the endeavors of locals in locally based cultural settings (Lederach 1997, 108–9). This is fundamentally different from the emancipatory approach of human security (Donais 2009, 6).

The second difference between the two concepts is who or what constitutes the adversary to people's empowerment. For the emancipatory approach of human security, due to the background of its emergence, liberal peacebuilding in the post-conflict period can be seen as an adversary of the "bottom-up" approach. "Peacebuilding from below" is a more complicated adversarial construct due to the fact that this concept is applied to all the conflict stages, not merely in the post-conflict period. During the pre- and in-conflict stages, injustice inside the country represents a target for the "bottom-up" concept. As a characteristic of intrastate conflict, a state

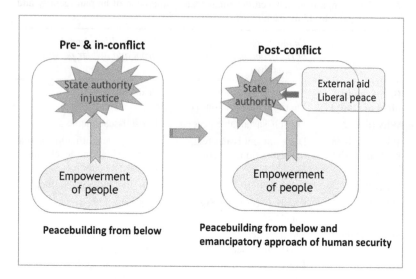

Figure 2.2 Empowerment of people in different phases of conflict

authority/government fails to protect its own population or even suppresses them. In this situation, locals need to empower themselves vis-à-vis the oppressing government or injustice. In the post-conflict situation, liberal peacebuilding is added as a further adversary for people's empowerment to be dealt with (see Figure 2.2).

It can be concluded that the emancipatory approach of human security and "peacebuilding from below" inherently share values, such as objectives, beneficiaries, and the importance of a "bottom-up" approach or empowerment of local people. They have slightly different points of view (from inside or outside conflict), however, as to when initially to empower locals. While "peacebuilding from below" places importance on self-empowerment within the native cultural setting, the emancipatory approach of human security takes it for granted that the third parties initially empower locals or, in a more moderate way, help the locals eventually empower themselves.

The next question is how to realize a self-sustainable peace through the "bottom-up" concept of human security, which both peacebuilding models have suggested. There have been a number of discussions on the obstacles to local ownership. The most orthodox argument is related to donor-driven peacebuilding (Krause and Jutersonke 2005), which seems to be a "chicken and egg" (which comes first) debate between the local ownership and liberal peace. The second argument, regarding assistance to "fragile states," concerns when international society should take over responsibility for a policy-making entity viewed as no longer capable of managing its own affairs. Hughes and Pupavac (2005, 883) call this the "pathologization of post-conflict societies" and locals are typically relegated to the role of grateful recipients. A third problem relates to different aspects of the peacebuilding time frame. The international community tends to have a "quickly fix and leave" mindset, although the reality of domestic processes is messy, unpredictable, and time-consuming. Under such circumstances, Donais (2009) points out the difficulty of engaging with local owners as an integral part of the peacebuilding endeavor, as it rarely produces immediately measurable results. Despite the difficulties, Donais maintains that local ownership can be deferred, but cannot ultimately be avoided.

A number of works have covered the question of local ownership, but little has been written in terms of the analysis of the specific identity of the relevant locals (Martin and Wilson 2008). Chesterman (2007) observes that in any post-conflict society, there is never a single coherent set of local owners and that post-conflict spaces are characterized far more by diversity and division than unity. The idea of "peacebuilding from below" is to empower local nongovernmental actors who are generally viewed as being more nonproblematically committed to peacebuilding. Civil society is often seen to carry the best hope for a genuine democratic counterweight to the powerbrokers, economic exploiters, and warlords who tend to predominate in conflict-ridden, weak, or failed states (Pouligny 2005, 496).

There has been no convincing body of evidence supporting the construction of self-sustainable peace, either only by local ownership or solely from the contributions of external actors. A third category of discourse, aside from the liberal approach and the "bottom-up" approach, has thus emerged to attempt to show the way to achieve self-sustainable peace through committed engagement of exogenous actors and endogenous communities. Donais (2009) has pointed out that developing methods to combine local and international resources in ways that maximize the long-term possibilities for sustainable peace remains one of the great challenges of contemporary peacebuilding.

It can be concluded, at this stage, that the concept of human security has connected peacebuilding and development to highlight local ownership or the "bottom-up" approach. With regard to the strategy of achieving a self-sustainable peace with local ownership, experts suggest a realistic solution, which is partnership between local ownership and external actors. This new approach lies beyond the debate of pro- or anti-liberal peacebuilding, although more empirical evidence is required in order to consolidate this new approach in academic discourses.

The following section attempts to combine elements of the discussions earlier in this chapter in order to articulate the concept of peacebuilding

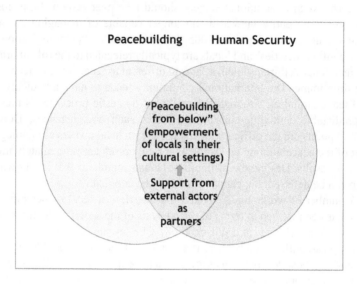

Figure 2.3 Peacebuilding and human security

through development from the perspective of human security. It does so in the hope of providing a foundation for the case studies from the ROK and Japan that will take place in the following chapters. First, in terms of peacebuilding from the perspective of human security, the overlap between peacebuilding and human security shown in Figure 2.3 is consistent with Lederach's "peacebuilding from below." In this model, local ownership is highlighted as a major engine for peacebuilding and external actors are expected to support local ownership in the local cultural settings.

Second, since the incorporation of peacebuilding into development studies research agendas in the post–Cold War era, the main focus has been on liberal peace and liberal peacebuilding, through the consideration of how external actors should engage with processes in the post-conflict period. The questionable durability of the externally driven policy reform is a key lesson learned from a half-century of international development assistance (Donais 2009, 10). There have been a number of development studies discussing pro- and anti-liberal peace. The "do no harm" principle is one of the very few anti-liberal peace theoretical approaches backed with empirical evidence. "Greed and grievance theory" also makes an appearance with regard to the causes of conflict, as shown in Figure 2.4.

Third, once Figure 2.3 and Figure 2.4 are combined, an intertwined concept between the three dimensions emerges, as shown in Figure 2.5. Segment (1) indicates a common issue among peacebuilding, human security,

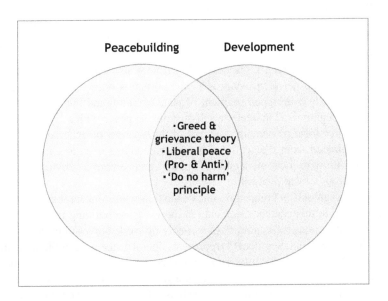

Figure 2.4 Peacebuilding and development

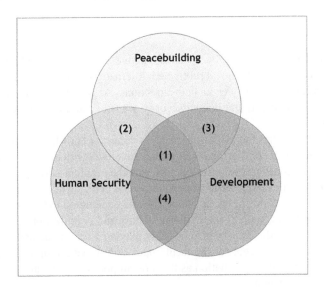

Figure 2.5 Peacebuilding nexus with human security and development

and development, which is the core focus of this chapter. When the perspective of human security is added to the discussion between peacebuilding and development, the emancipatory approach of human security emerges, emphasizing local ownership from the viewpoint of external actors. The discussion of Lederach's "peacebuilding from below" has also focused on the relationship between locals and external actors once the development facet joins the overlapped segment of peacebuilding and human security. In short, Segment (1) indicates a self-sustainable peace with a "bottom-up" approach or local ownership. The role of third parties or external actors is not eliminated from the segment, but external actors need to enter a new partnership with local ownership to support and cement a self-sustainable peace through local ownership.

Other segments in Figure 2.5 indicate the following concepts based on the discussion in this chapter. Segment (2) shows "peacebuilding from below" without development factors. Problem-solving workshops and training can fall in this segment. Segment (3) represents liberal peace/peacebuilding with the Western models for modernization, especially introduction of democracy, human rights, and a market economy. Segment (4) can accommodate endogenous development theory as well as self-reliance and empowerment theory, which have been discussed in development studies since the 1970s. Segment (1)+(2) is identical to what has been discussed – the nexus between peacebuilding and human security, which is "peacebuilding from below."

Conclusion

Contemporary conflicts, by their distinctive nature, are predominantly multi-faceted, intrastate, and protracted. International, national, and human insecurities can spill over in both directions. At the same time, conflict/ peace, development, and human security are connected in a complex web of causality.

This chapter has found that, based on the concept of positive peace, Azar's protracted social conflict theory legitimates the involvement of development as a tool for conflict resolution together with the problem-solving approach. In his theory, however, the local population was depicted not as actors but as beneficiaries. At this point, development was understood to be provided by external players, such as international donors and organizations, with top-level leaders in the country also possibly playing a role. Lederach reversed the beneficiary concept for the local population in peacebuilding. Instead, he regards the local population as the most important actors and advocates their empowerment.

Lederach's focus on people and local communities allowed him to reframe his peacebuilding theory to focus on the concept of conflict transformation.

Peacebuilding, in view of conflict transformation, is not merely post-conflict reconstruction but continuous endeavors in pre- and in-conflict situations as well. Since conflict transformation is rooted in local efforts in their cultural settings, the role of third parties should be as partners of local actors. The concept of conflict transformation has evolved to include the perspective of human security. Hence, this chapter has moved on to address the intertwined relationships among human security, development, and peacebuilding.

Because of the perceived Western-centric nature of the liberal peace, and a number of failed examples of liberal peacebuilding, the matter of local ownership has been placed under the spotlight and the emancipatory approach of human security has emerged to place local ownership in the center of peacebuilding. At the same time, as mentioned above, the rapidly shifting nature of peacebuilding and development cooperation in the 21st century has enabled new proactive policy-making among non-Western middle powers.

The chapter has found significant commonalities between the concepts of "peacebuilding from below" and the emancipatory approach, for which human security has functioned as an intermediary. Both of the concepts share the value of a "bottom-up" approach through empowerment of locals as the key to successful peacebuilding – although they employ different initial approaches to empowerment of locals. Aside from local ownership as a key factor for successful peacebuilding, the chapter has looked at ways of achieving a self-sustainable peace – in other words, the question of how to regard external actors for peacebuilding within the framework of local ownership. While a self-sustainable peace with the bottom-up approach or local ownership has become the central idea, the role of third parties or external actors has not been eliminated. External actors need to enter into new partnerships with local ownership to support and solidify self-sustaining peace.

Development studies have shown a new direction for peacebuilding – a partnership between local ownership and external actors. This is also in harmony with the concept of "peacebuilding from below." On the conceptual level, this new partnership can be interpreted as implying that external actors are expected to support local ownership in local cultural settings. In order to prove the effectiveness of this concept, however, the accumulation and review of evidence on the ground is indispensable.

External assistance can facilitate the building of peace, development, and human security within fragile communities. Peaceful environments can facilitate the construction of both development and human security. The building of lasting peace requires consideration of the distribution of well-being through development, and the human security of the most vulnerable sections of society. Human security includes consideration of freedom from fear (facilitated through the building of peace), freedom from want (facilitated through development and distributive justice), and freedom to live in dignity, which is best ensured through empowerment. The key factor running through all of these paradigms is the importance of human agency – peacebuilding from below, human development, and the notion of distributive justice, which emphasizes benefits to the least well-off and, of course, the prioritization of human rather than state security.

While exogenous agencies can contribute to all three perspectives by assisting one, failure to consider the complexities of the relationships between them, or a failure to focus on human agency and endogenous empowerment could have negative or counter-productive consequences. Thus, focusing solely on peacebuilding from the top down can contribute to future sources of conflict emanating from the inequality and vulnerability experienced by some individuals and groups. Focusing solely on development can undermine peace due to relative deprivation, while at the same time contributing to the human insecurity of the most vulnerable. Focusing on national security can undermine peace through the security dilemma, while also diverting resources from development, and undermine human security through the processes described in this chapter.

The subsequent chapters, therefore, will assess the contributions of Japanese and South Korean governments in overseas assistance policy-making from the perspective of the impacts they have across the whole paradigmatic landscape, but with particular attention paid to human agency and empowerment. This will also be the perspective taken for policy prescription. Finally, the concluding chapter will consider the extent to which synergy of approaches between the niche diplomacy of these two middle powers can spill over to an improvement of relations between the two countries.

References

Acharya, A. (2002) "Human security: What kind for the Asia Pacific?" in Dickens, D. ed., *The Human Face of Security: Asia-Pacific Perspectives* Australian National University Press, Canberra 5–17.

Anderson, M. (1999) *Do No Harm: How Aid Can Support Peace-or War* Lynne Rienner Publishers, Boulder.

Azar, E. E. (1983) "The theory of protracted social conflict and the challenge of transforming conflict situations" *Monograph Series in World Affairs* 20(2) 81–99.

——— (1990) *The Management of Protracted Social Conflict: Theory and Cases* Dartmouth Pub, Aldershot.

Ballentine, K. and Nitzchke, H. (2003) "Beyond greed and grievances: Policy lessons from studies in the political economy of armed conflict" in *IPA Policy Report* International Peace Academy, New York.

Begby, E. and Burgess, J. P. (2009) "Human security and liberal peace" *Public Reason* 1(1) 91–104.

Boulding, K. (1961) *Perspectives on the Economics of Peace* Institute for International Orders, New York.

———— (1962) *Conflict and Defense* Harper and Row, New York.

Boutros-Ghali, B. (1992) *An Agenda for Peace: Preventive Diplomacy, Peacemaking and Peacekeeping* Report of the UN Secretary-General, A/47/277-S/24111.

Burton, J. W. (1987) *Resolving Deep-Rooted Conflict: A Handbook* University Press of America, Lanhan, MD.

———— ed. (1990) *Conflict: Human Needs Theory* St. Martin's Press, New York.

Calder, K. (1988) "Japanese foreign economic policy formation: Explaining the reactive state" *World Politics* 40(4) 517–41.

———— (2005) "Halfway to hegemony: Japan's tortured trajectory" *Harvard International Review* 27(3) 46–9.

Chesterman, S. (2007) "Ownership in theory and in practice: Transfer of authority in UN statebuilding operations" *Journal of Intervention and Statebuilding* 1(1) 3–26.

Cline, R. (1977) *World Power Assessment: A Calculus of Strategic Drift* Westview Press, Boulder.

Collier, P. (2000) *Economic Causes of Civil Conflict and Their Implications for Policy* World Bank, Washington, DC.

Curle, A. (1971) *Making Peace* Tavistock, London.

———— (1986) *In the Middle: Non-Official Mediation in Violent Situations* Berg, Oxford.

Diamond, L. and McDonald, J. W. (1996) *Multi-Track Diplomacy: A Systems Approach to Peace* Kumarian Press, Boulder.

Donais, T. (2009) "Empowerment or imposition? Dilemmas of local ownership in post-conflict peacebuilding processes" *Peace & Change* 34(1) 3–26.

Dorn, J. (1998) "Competing visions of development policy" in Dorn, J., Hanks, S. and Walters, A. eds., *The Revolution in Development Economics* Cato Institute, Washington, DC.

Fisher, R. J. (1993) "The potential for peacebuilding: Forging a bridge from peacekeeping to peacemaking" *Peace and Change* 18(3) 247–66.

———— (1997) *Interactive Conflict Resolution* Syracuse University Press, New York.

Galtung, J. (1969) "Conflict as a way of life" in Freeman, H. ed., *Progress in Mental Health* Churchill, London.

———— (1990) "Cultural violence" *Journal of Peace Research* 27(3) 291–305.

Geneva International Centre for Humanitarian Demining (GICHD) (2007) *Lao PDR Risk Management and Mitigation Model* GICHD, Geneva.

Gorman, E. (2011) *Conflict and Development* Zed Books, New York.

Haas, E. (1958) *The Uniting of Europe: Political, Social, and Economic Forces, 1950–1957* Stanford University Press, Stanford.

———— (1964) *Beyond the Nation-State: Functionalism and International Organization* Stanford University Press, Stanford.

Harvey, D. (2005) *A Brief History of Neoliberalism* Oxford University Press, Oxford.

Hirata, K. (1998) "Japan as a reactivist state? Analyzing Japan's relations with the Socialist Republic of Vietnam" *Japanese Studies* 18(2) 1–31.

Homer-Dixon, T. (1994) "Environmental scarcities and violent conflict: Evidence from cases" *International Security* 19(1) 5–40.

Howe, B. (2017a) "Korea's role for peace-building and development in Asia" *Asian Journal of Peacebuilding* 5(2) 243–66.

——— (2017b) "Challenges and opportunities for South Korean diplomacy in an era of new varieties of power and influence" *Korean Journal of Security Affairs* 22(1) 4–22.

Hughes, C. and Pupavac, V. (2005) "Framing post-conflict societies: International pathologisation of Cambodia and the post-Yugoslav states" *Third World Quarterly* 26(6) 873–89.

Jeong, H. (2000) *Peace and Conflict Studies: An Introduction* Ashgate Publishing Ltd, Aldershot.

Kalinowski, T. and Cho, H. (2012) "Korea's search for a global role between hard economic interests and soft power" *European Journal of Development Research* 24(2) 242–60.

Kelman, H. (1992) "Informal mediation by the scholar/practitioner" in Bercovitch, J., and Rubin, J. Z. eds., *Mediation in International Relations* St. Martin's Press, New York 64–96.

——— (1996) "The interactive problem solving approach" in Crocker, C. A, and Hampson F. O. eds., *Managing Global Chaos: Sources of and Responses to International Conflict* US Institute of Peace Press, Washington, DC 500–20.

Krause, K. and Jutersonke, O. (2005) "Peace, security and development in post-conflict environments" *Security Dialogue* 36(4) 447–62.

Lal, D. (1998) "The transformation of developing economies: From plan to market" in Dorn, J., Hanks, S. and Walters, A. eds., *The Revolution in Development Economics* Cato Institute, Washington, DC 55–74.

Lederach, J. P. (1997) *Building Peace* United States Institute of Peace, Washington, DC.

——— (1999) *The Journey toward Reconciliation* Herald Press, Scottdale.

Lee, S. (2014) "South Korea's middle power diplomacy: Multilayered world order and the case of development cooperation policy" *EAI MPDI Working Paper* East Asian Institute, Seoul (www.eai.or.kr/data/bbs/eng_report/2014102816225492. pdf) Accessed July 12, 2018.

Mac Ginty, R. and Williams, A. (2016) *Conflict and Development* Routledge, Oxon.

Martin, A. and Wilson, P. (2008) "Security sector evolution: Which locals? Ownership of what?" in Donais, T. ed., *Local Ownership and Security Sector Reform* Geneva Centre for the Democratic Control of Armed Forces, Geneva 83–103.

Ministry of National Defence (MND) (2015) *Defence White Paper 2014* (www. mnd.go.kr/user/mnd/upload/pblictn/PBLICTNEBOOK_201501060619270840. pdf) Accessed July 12, 2018.

Mitrany, D. (1933) *The Progress of International Government* Yale University Press, New Haven.

Mogami, S. (2006) *Ima heiwa to wa: Jinken to jindou we meguru kyu-wa [What Is Peace: Nine Stories about Human Rights and Humanity]* Iwanami Shinsho, Tokyo.

Montville, J. V. (1987) "The arrow and the olive branch: A case for track two diplomacy in conflict resolution" in McDonald, J. W. and Bendahman, D. B. eds., *Track Two Diplomacy* Foreign Service Institute, Washington, DC 161–75.

Musoni, P. (2003) *Innovations in Governance and Public Administration for Poverty Reduction in Post-Conflict Countries in a Globalised World* (http://unpan1.un.org/intradoc/groups/public/documents/un/unpan007601.pdf) Accessed July 12, 2018.

Newman, E., Paris, R., and Richmond, O. (2009) *New Perspectives on Liberal Peacebuilding* United Nations University Press, Tokyo.

Peterson, J. (2009) "Creating space for emancipatory human security: Liberal obstructions and the potential of agonism" *Center of International Relations Working Paper* 51(September)

Pouligny, B. (2005) "Civil society and post-conflict peacebuilding: Ambiguities of international programmes aimed at building 'new' societies" *Security Dialogue* 36(4) 495–510.

Ramsbotham, O., Woodhouse, T., and Miall, H. eds. (2005) *Contemporary Conflict Resolution* 2nd Edition Polity Press, Cambridge.

Richmond, O. (2006) "The problem of peace: Understanding the liberal peace" *Conflict, Security & Development* 6(3) 291–314.

————— (2007) "Emancipatory forms of human security and liberal peacebuilding" *International Journal* 62(3) 459–77.

Sen, A. (2006) *Identity and Violence* Norton, New York.

Soeya, Y. (2005) "Japanese security policy in transition: The rise of international and human security" *Asia-Pacific Review* 12(1) 103–16.

Statistics Times (2016) *Projected GDP Ranking (2016–2020)* December 16 (http://statisticstimes.com/economy/projected-world-gdp-ranking.php) Accessed July 12, 2018.

Stockholm International Peace Research Institute (SIPRI) (2017) *Trends in World Military Expenditure, 2016* (www.sipri.org/sites/default/files/Trends-world-military-expenditure-2016.pdf) Accessed July 12, 2018.

Suh, J. J. (2013) "Rethinking national and human security in North Korea" in Park, K. A. ed., *Non-Traditional Security Issues in North Korea* University of Hawaii Press, Honolulu 1–22.

Tadjbakhsh, S. (2010) "Human security and the legitimisation of peacebuilding" in Richmond, O. ed., *Palgrave Advances in Peacebuilding: Critical Developments and Approaches* Palgrave Macmillan, Basingstoke 116–36.

Taira, K. (1991) "Japan an imminent hegemon?" *Annals of the American Academy of Political and Social Science* 513(1) 151–63.

Tellis, A., Bially, J., Layne, C., and McPherson, M. (2000) *Measuring Power in the Postindustrial Age* RAND, Santa Monica.

Tirman, J. (2015) "The human costs of war: And how to assess the damage" *Foreign Affairs* October 8 (www.foreignaffairs.com/articles/middle-east/2015-10-08/human-cost-war) Accessed July 12, 2018.

United Nations (UN) (2008) *The Millennium Development Goals Report* (www.un.org/millenniumgoals/2008highlevel/pdf/newsroom/mdg%20reports/MDG_Report_2008_ENGLISH.pdf) Accessed July 12, 2018.

United Nations Development Programme (UNDP) (2015) "What is human development?" (http://hdr.undp.org/en/content/what-human-development) Accessed July 4, 2018.

——— (2016) "Issue brief: Development and mine action" (www.undp.org/content/undp/en/home/librarypage/poverty-reduction/development-and-mine-action-policy-and-programming.html) Accessed July 12, 2018.

Unger, D. C. (2012) *The Emergency State: America's Pursuit of Absolute Security at All Costs* The Penguin Press, New York.

Wæver, O. (1995) "Securitization and desecuritization" in Lipschutz, R. D. ed., *On Security* Columbia University Press, New York 46–86.

Wallensteen, P. (2007) *Understanding Conflict Resolution* 2nd Edition Sage Pub, London.

Watson, A. (2004) *An Introduction to International Political Economy* Continuum, London.

Woodhouse, T. (2010) "Adam Curle: Radical peacemaker and pioneer of peace studies" *Journal of Conflictology* 1(1) 1–7.

3 Human fragility in Southeast Asia

The CLMV countries and the Philippines[1]

Suyoun Jang

Introduction

Since 2001, the international development community has been paying increased attention to the global security and development challenges posed by fragile states. Fragile states, which have been described as "the toughest development challenge of our era" (Zoellick 2008, 68), "the single most important problem for international order" (Fukuyama 2004, 92), and "the main security challenge of our time" (Gates 2010), have come to the forefront of the policy and research arenas. While the terms "fragile state" and "fragility" are now widely used, and the academic literature on the concepts and classification has grown rapidly, there is still no generally agreed definition of either. Each country, organization, and scholar has developed its own view on what counts as a fragile state, and many related notions are also used such as failed, failing, weak, or collapsed, without any precise change in meaning (Cammack et al. 2006, 16).

Nonetheless, "fragile states" appears to be the most popular term to encompass the variety of notions that denote a country that is either unable or unwilling to fulfill its basic responsibilities to protect and provide. Accordingly, the British Department for International Development (DFID) defines fragile states as those "where the government cannot or will not deliver core functions to the majority of its people" (DFID 2005, 7). The Organization for Economic Cooperation and Development (OECD) similarly defines fragile states as countries that "lack political will and/or capacity to provide the basic functions needed for poverty reduction, development and to safeguard the security and human rights of their populations" (OECD 2007, 2).

At the same time, the definition can go beyond a government's failure to provide security and basic services to include weak governance institutions, authority and legitimacy failures, accountability gaps, and high levels of volatility. For example, Canada's Country Indicators for Foreign Policy (CIFP) project extends the definition of fragile states to include the functional authority to provide security within their borders, and the political legitimacy to effectively represent their citizens at home or abroad (CIFP 2006). The US Agency for International Development (USAID) similarly defines fragile states as countries where the legitimacy of the government is weak or nonexistent (USAID 2005, 1).

The loosely defined, and hence analytically weak, nature of the fragile states concept is a disturbing feature, especially from a policy-oriented perspective (Bertoli and Ticci 2012, 212). Different underlying definitions of and criteria for fragile states can lead to countries being identified as fragile for different reasons. As a consequence, countries will be unable to develop adequate instruments to deal with the problems posed by all the varieties of fragility. The label itself can also be a source of contention, especially when the term is used to "name and shame" a country with weak institutions. Most importantly, the state-level focus can neglect regional variations in fragility within a state. Nonetheless, while the debate continues on the use of the term, the concept of fragility remains useful as it refers to places, systems, and situations where caution should be applied to strategic planning and special care taken with program and project design (Jang and Milante 2016, 354).

Against this backdrop, this chapter proposes a new conceptual and analytical framework for fragility analysis of human fragility. This human fragility framework is intended to complement, rather than replace, the current state-centered frameworks by placing subnational variations in the scale of violence, the existence of marginalized and excluded groups, and levels of poverty at the center of fragility analysis. To this end, it first examines recent shifts in approaches to the study of fragility and alternative notions relevant to the new framework, such as vulnerability, resilience, and human security. The human fragility framework is developed building on this review. The chapter then assesses human fragility with a specific focus on Southeast Asia.

From state fragility to human fragility

Non-state-centric approach to fragility

The state still serves a useful analytical purpose. Most donor countries and international organizations working in the development field have country-based operational models and allocation systems. They primarily work at the state level to support fragile states in their transition out of poverty and fragility. Collecting data, monitoring, and evaluation are conducted to help a state improve its development performance and achieve better outcomes. The statist approach, however, always begins from the assumption that the state is a distinct entity from society, albeit that the line between the two is uncertain (Mitchell 1991, 89). It also assumes a uniformity in state organization, structure, and behavior that ignores, misunderstands, and devalues alternative forms of governance which might function differently than assumed (Leander 2009, 8). Hence, a state-level focus can omit more important information about how development and fragility affect society and people, and how fragility differs over space and causes geographical disparities.

As a result, there have been a growing number of attempts to analyze fragility from a non-state-centric perspective. For example, Naudé, McGillivray, and Rossow (2009) examined spatial inequalities in various socioeconomic domains to show how fragility can exist at the local level in states that are generally considered stable. Guo and Freeman (2011) studied regional fragility in the border areas between countries. A number of authors have explored customary authorities and institutions in fragile states, for example para-sovereign zones of rule (Adalbert Hampel 2015) or hybrid political orders (Boege, Brown, and Clements 2009). They found that such non-state actors are not necessarily "spoilers," but potential sources of solutions when it comes to building peace and constructive state-society relations. This approach has shed new light on the importance of taking local context, local actors, and subnational governance into account, and hence opened up new options for state and peacebuilding to take a bottom-up approach (Brinkerhoff 2011; Kaplan 2010; Lederach 1997, 1999).

At the same time, however, some have found a solution to state fragility in state-society relations, on the basis that the state is embedded in, not independent of, society. Pouligny (2010) refers to strong state-society relations as one of the "intangible" dimensions of state resilience and state building, and calls on the international aid community to integrate local societies and communities into their aid programs in order to rebuild a functioning and supportive state-society relationship. Similarly, the 2011 World Development Report emphasized restoring confidence and trust between societal groups, and between state and society by mobilizing "inclusive-enough" coalitions in order to prevent violence and conflict, and consequently to transform institutions (World Bank 2011). In addition, Alexander et al. (2013, 13) claim that fragility is a problem not just of state capacity, but also of dysfunctional relationships among groups in society, including the relationships different groups have with the state. In this sense, fostering social cohesion that translates into more effective institutions will be important for moving away from or avoiding fragile situations.

More recently, as rapid urbanization has exacerbated fragility in large and intermediate cities, attention has focused on such cities (de Boer 2015; Muggah 2013). Fragile cities, host to an increasing number of informal settlements and migrants, are experiencing crises of urban governance, and have become prone to extreme violence, and vulnerable to disaster and poverty. They have emerged as the "epicenter of vulnerability," with severe humanitarian and military implications (Graham 2010; Lucchi 2013; Muggah and Savage 2012; Nogueira 2017). Nogueira (2017), in particular, has redefined humanitarian space at the city level by tracing the shift in fragility discourse along with the changes in the settings where risk and vulnerability reside. He places urban areas above the state as the primary object of humanitarian action by arguing that the term "fragility" is not confined to describing a state's willingness or capacity, but also used to characterize "zones" and "areas" that are vulnerable to the risk of violence, disaster, and other crises.

This non-state-centric focus on fragility brings about an analytical transition to a framework that highlights the dynamics of multiple dimensions of fragility and brings the analysis closer to the most vulnerable part of a fragile state. It also raises the issue of whether people, rather than the state, should be the focus of development, since state development is not always accompanied by social and human development, while a state's fragility is a grave impediment to the latter. State-society relations provide a good example of how the problem of and solutions to fragility can be understood at the non-state level by making society the key element underpinning state institutions, legitimacy, and capacity. Paying attention to people in fragile settings, however, is still largely neglected, and falls into other strands of the literature.

Vulnerability, resilience, and human security

Non-state-centric analyses are more visible in the literature on vulnerability and resilience. Both terms are widely used in a variety of fields and have different foci and meanings. The concept of vulnerability was developed largely in the social sciences to address environmental risks and hazards (Kasperson et al. 2005; Wisner et al. 2003). It is generally defined as the "susceptibility of a system to harm due to exposure to a hazard(s)" (Adger 2006). Vulnerability is a core concept in disaster risk management and the study of livelihoods and poverty, food security, and climate change (Miller et al. 2010). Such research commonly focuses on the most vulnerable and marginalized groups, which face unequal exposure to risks, and examines the underlying causes or determinants of vulnerability that generate this inequality. The relationships between risks and the ways in which human systems place people at risk are understood as an individual's, a household's, a community's, or a society's vulnerability. Vulnerability, therefore, often relates to an undesirable outcome, such as vulnerability to poverty or natural disaster, whereas "positive vulnerability" refers to cases where crises become "windows of opportunity" in which even negative events that have destructive effects can produce positive outcomes (Gallopín 2006, 295).

Resilience, on the other hand, emerged from ecological science to address persistence and change in ecosystems, but was subsequently expanded to other research fields (Berkes 2007; Nelson, Adger, and Brown 2007; Zou and Thomalla 2008). It refers to the "capacity of a system to absorb disturbance and reorganize while undergoing change so as to still retain essentially the same function, structure, identity, and feedbacks" (Walker et al. 2004). According to this definition, resilience is about (a) returning to a previous state, so-called equilibrium, following disturbance; and (b) being robust or persistent during the disturbance so as to maintain certain desirable system characteristics despite fluctuations in the behavior of component parts of the environment. In this regard, research has been carried out to examine, for example, social and institutional responses to climate change and solutions for livelihood recovery (Boyd et al. 2008; Osbahr et al. 2008; Thomas et al. 2007).

A more straightforward non-state-centric approach can be found in human security research. The human security perspective purports to focus on individuals as the referent object of security, and to explore threats to human survival, safety, and dignity. The human security literature has bifurcated into freedom from fear and freedom from want. Freedom from fear stresses individual safety and security from physical threats and, therefore, highlights the dangers to citizens that arise from endemic violence and conflict (ICISS 2001; Ignatieff 2002). Freedom from want focuses on the socioeconomic challenges facing people in fragile settings (Branchflower 2004). Others have taken a more synthetic approach, identifying a vicious cycle in human security and national security (Agamben 2005; Jensen 2010; Orjuela 2010; Stedman and Tanner 2003), and that connections can increasingly be found in situations where neither security nor development is attainable in isolation, that is, in fragile states (Stern and Öjendal 2010).

Although many have been critical of the concept of human security,[2] the approach remains valuable because of its ability to highlight threats to relatively unprotected individuals and groups in fragile states (Carment, Prest, and Samy 2010, 15). Furthermore, the concept of a fragile state is useful insofar as state fragility is understood in relation to its citizens, who are directly affected by and living with state failure, and will also have to cope with its aftermath (Bøås and Jennings 2005). This raises an important question about "who the state is fragile for," rather than "which state is fragile," and highlights the consequences of state fragility as they are experienced by individuals. Thus, state fragility, as the basis for investigations into human security, can be defined as the extent to which a state is able or willing to function in a manner conducive to the welfare and security of its citizens, and the conditions and context in which state action or inaction occurs (Bøås and Jennings 2005, 390).

What is human fragility?

Defining human fragility

A human fragility framework seeks to replace the focus on the state with an examination of subnational or transnational areas of vulnerability in order to fill the gaps left by the state-centric approach. It aims to explore the situations of fragility in which institutions – both state and non-state – have insufficient capacity to deal with human fragility or otherwise create a sustainable environment for human development. The focus on human fragility, therefore, takes place in the context of increasing contestation in the state-centric fragility framework and emerges from the problematization of fragility as a measure of the vulnerability of people.

A human fragility framework has following features. First, the concept of human fragility incorporates the notion of human security, where security is seen as freedom from existential threat to the referent object. This means that human security relates vulnerability to individuals and makes them a normative and empirical reference point (Nuscheler, Debiel, and Messner 2007, 16). In this sense, human security is deliberately protective. While many have tried to identify and cluster threats to human security or devise indicators to measure it, this study does not specify the types of threat to human security (King and Christopher 2001; Madrueño-Aguilar 2016; UN 2004; UNDP 1994). This is partly because human security is people-centered rather than threat-centered, and partly because such threats are mutually reinforcing and interconnected, and hence any attempt to prioritize one type of threat over another would be artificial (OCHA 2009). Instead of identifying and prioritizing threats to human security, the focus is put on the core value of protecting the most vulnerable. The most vulnerable in this context refers to those who are exposed to immediate physical threats to life or deprived of life-sustaining resources (Suhrke 1999).

Second, the framework highlights not only the negative consequences of, but also susceptibility to experiencing human insecurity. This reflects the fact that people can demonstrate the capacity to cope and bounce back after threats, and that their non-victimhood deserves to be acknowledged (Cannon 2008, 9). In social systems, however, resilience does not aim for a static equilibrium. Instead, a dynamic process of communications and interactions leads to constant changes in structures, institutions, and social relations. When a social system encounters shocks, it seeks not just to bounce back to pre-shock status, but to improve its functionality and maintain these improvements. In this sense, resilience is rather like "negative peace," in which the imminent threat of violence is eliminated but the "shadow of the future" still looms large (Milante 2017, 215). Positive peace, by contrast, which is positioned at the other end of the spectrum in Figure 3.1, is a self-sustaining and thriving peace, and one that is collaborative, inclusive, and based on mutual trust, which therefore makes

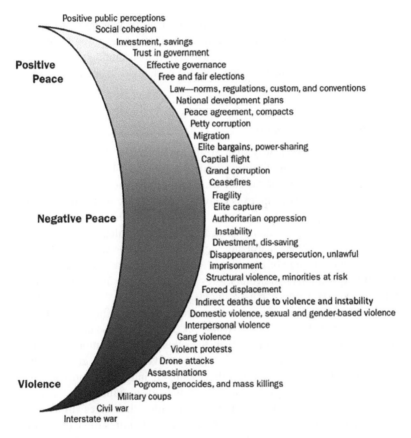

Figure 3.1 A violence–peace spectrum and manifestations of violence and peace

Source: Milante (2017, 216).

Note: The examples of violence, negative peace, and positive peace shown in the figure are not meant to be cardinal, ordinal, or complete. They are themselves outcomes and indicative of the quality of the peace.

sustainable social and human development possible. In the same vein, Taleb (2012) refers to "antifragility," which is beyond resilience, as the other end of the fragility continuum that describes post-shock growth and development. Therefore, unlike the general understanding of resilience as the opposite of fragility or vulnerability, this study uses the terms "antifragility" and "positive peace," which are beyond resilience, as the ultimate goals to be reached in tackling human fragility.

Thus, this study attempts to develop a synthetic framework that integrates vulnerability, positive peace/antifragility, and human security to define human fragility as a

> situation or place where people are insecure or vulnerable to becoming insecure. People are insecure when they are exposed to immediate physical threats to life or deprived of life-sustaining resources, and vulnerable when they do not have the capacity to respond to physical threats or deprivation.

Measuring human fragility

Current approaches identify many different criteria and countless indicators for measuring state fragility. Table 3.1 lists the 14 existing analytical frameworks on fragile states and compares their various aims, attributes, and limitations. Various indexes converge around a combination of social, economic, governance, and security factors as measures of state fragility. Most provide country rankings on an annual basis by calculating the average scores obtained by standardizing, aggregating, and/or weighting the values of each dimension of fragility. In addition to national or internationally available quantitative indicators, they use qualitative indicators obtained through expert surveys and assessments.

The lists and rankings can draw attention to the most fragile countries at the top of the list (Milante and Woolcock 2017). It is less clear, however, which country is more fragile than the others, and thus more in need of more assistance, in the mid-table rankings. Even with the group of most fragile countries (if identified), the wealth of indicators and categories and the method of aggregation make it difficult to gain a precise understanding of the most pressing types of fragility challenges. In addition, even where there seems to be agreement on the features of state fragility, there is less consensus on which of these features are root causes, which are symptoms, and where the pathways into and out of state fragility lie (Brinkerhoff 2011, 135).

Similarly, and even more importantly, the aggregation process can give rise to the problem of assumed compensation (Gutiérrez Sanín 2009, 2011;

Table 3.1 Comparison of state fragility approaches

Index	Coverage	Purpose	Dimensions	Methodology	Results
Bertelsmann Transformation Index (BTI)	129 countries excluding long-consolidated democratic systems and advanced economies	To evaluate the performance of developing countries and countries in transition	Political, economic, management	Calibrate and standardize the scores attained by country experts' assessments	Country rankings of the Status Index and the Transformation Index
CIFP Fragility Index	For 2016, 199 countries	To develop a tool and methodology to evaluate, assess, address challenges, and causes of fragility	Authority, Legitimacy, and Capacity (ALC) with seven sub-dimensions	Unweighted average score of all indicators	Scores for the ALC, scores for the seven sub-dimensions and composite index with cross-country rankings
Fragile States Index	All recognized sovereign states with sufficient data. For 2017, 178 countries	To identify the degree to which countries risk state failure	Social, economic, political	Based on the Conflict Assessment System Tool (CAST) analytical approach, triangulates data from content analysis, quantitative data, and qualitative review	Country rankings

(*Continued*)

Table 3.1 (Continued)

Index	Coverage	Purpose	Dimensions	Methodology	Results
Global Peace Index	163 countries	To measure negative peace: absence of (threat of) violence	Security, governance	Sum of the weighted scores from 23 indicators on internal peace and external peace	Overall peacefulness scores by countries and associated global and regional rankings
Harmonized List of Fragile Situations	For 2017, 35 countries	To allocate aid by the World Bank and the regional development banks	Economic, social, security, governance	CPIA scores based on the expert assessments of World Bank staff	CPIA scores and fragile states list
Ibrahim Index of African Governance (IIAG)	For 2017, all 54 African countries	To evaluate country performance in Africa	Economic, social, security, governance	100 indicators on performance from 36 sources	IIAG scores, ranks, and trends
Index of State Weakness in the Developing World	141 developing countries (population > 100,000)	To advance policy and research on fragility by better understanding and operationalization	Economic, social, security, governance	Averages of 20 indicators on state weakness	State weakness scores and country rankings
International Country Risk Guide	140 countries in developing and emerging regions of the world	To manage risk for businesses	Economic, social, security, governance	22 variables in three subcategories: political risk (50% weight), financial risk (25% weight), and economic risk (25% weight)	Separate index for each subcategory, and composite country scores and rankings

International Futures (IFs) Governance Model	Model variables have been employed in empirical analyses	To forecast state trajectories	Economic, social, security, governance	Unweighted averages of indicators and sub-indices	Indices by dimensions and overall governance index
Peace and Conflict Instability Ledger	For 2012, 163 countries	To understand and predict instability	Economic, social, security, governance	Global model of risk prediction using data from 1950 to 2003 and from the most recent three years	Overall risk scores and scores for each risk dimension
Pillars of Peace	162 countries	To identify peace drivers	Economic, social, security, governance	Eight categories of peace factors based on data from 20 sources	Correlation scores between pillars of peace and peace
Political Instability Index	165 countries (2007 and 2009 rankings)	To predict instability onset	Economic, social, security, governance	Two indexes form the overall scores of underlying vulnerability and economic distress	Instability scores by country as average performance
State Fragility Index	Sovereign countries (population > 500,000), for 2016, 167 countries	To compare fragility research	Economic, social, security, governance	Effectiveness and legitimacy scores are calculated for each dimension based on quantitative data	Fragility scores and rankings
Worldwide Governance Indicators	Over 200 countries or territories from 1996 onwards	To compare governance over time and space	Economic, social, security, governance	Hundreds of variables from 31 sources capturing governance perception	Country performance scores and rankings of six governance dimensions

Ziaja 2012). Aggregation proceeds as if there is a common standard by which value is computed. This allows decision makers to count how many units of variable "A" substitute or compensate for one unit of variable "B." This means that aggregation may allow for a deterioration in one variable, such as child mortality, to compensate for an improvement in another one, such as the level of corruption. Assumptions about substitution rates between variables – often in the absence of any theoretical basis to back them up – are even more difficult to sustain in the context of social and political databases. Therefore, the country rankings are "fully" arbitrary, unless the aggregation function is transparent and can be tested (Gutiérrez Sanín 2009).

Furthermore, different fragility rankings do not correspond well with each other. Table 3.2 compares the 40 worst performing countries according to the five most widely used measurements of state fragility: the Fragile States Index (Messner et al. 2017), the Harmonized List of Fragile Situations (World Bank 2016), the State Fragility Index (Marshall and Elzinga-Marshall 2017), the Bertelsmann Transformation Index (BTI) (Bertelsmann Stiftung 2016), and the Country Indicators for Foreign Policy Fragility Index (Carment et al. 2017). This group of five indexes is selected for comparison based on: impact; similarities in conceptualization; purpose and measurement dimensions; and data availability.[3] A quick glance shows that no country is consistently ranked in the bottom five across all indexes, six countries are found in the bottom ten across all the indexes,[4] and 15 countries are common to all approaches.[5] There are 58 countries that appear in just one of the five lists. Furthermore, the table reflects the (sometimes incoherent) grouping of countries in the State Fragility Index and the BTI. For example, Laos is grouped with Zimbabwe under the BTI, but with Bangladesh, Djibouti, Egypt, Equatorial Guinea, Kyrgyzstan, the Philippines, and Zambia in the State Fragility Index.

Table 3.3 lists the countries that are unique to each list of fragile states. On the Harmonized List, these are mostly small island states and small economies. The BTI includes a number of countries in the Middle East and Latin America that are not included on other lists. Table 3.4 lists countries that are notably absent from a particular list but included on more than two other lists. For example, the Harmonized List does not include Angola, Cameroon, the Republic of the Congo (Congo), Ethiopia, Mauritania, and Pakistan, which are included on the other fragile state lists.

These inconsistent groupings reflect the complexities and difficulties of reducing multidimensional fragility to a one-dimensional measurement (Gutiérrez Sanín 2011). Using distinct analytical frameworks also poses the inherent problem of a lack of policy coherence, resulting in disparate policy prescriptions (Carment, Prest, and Samy 2010). It is even more unclear what

Table 3.2 Comparison of the fragile states rankings

Rank	Fragile States Index 2017	Harmonized List FY 2017	State Fragility Index 2016	BTI 2016	CIFP Fragility Index 2016
1	South Sudan	Somalia	DRC	Somalia	South Sudan
2	Somalia	South Sudan	Central African Rep.	Eritrea	Chad
3	Central African Rep.	Eritrea	South Sudan	Syria	Somalia
4	Yemen	Sudan	Sudan	North Korea	Central African Rep.
5	Sudan	Central African Rep.	Afghanistan	Sudan	Yemen
6	Syria	Guinea-Bissau	Burundi	Libya	Eritrea
7	DRC	Marshall Islands	Yemen	South Sudan	Sudan
8	Chad	Yemen	Somalia	Central African Rep.	Mali
9	Afghanistan	Afghanistan	Chad	Yemen	Afghanistan
10	Iraq	Micronesia	Ethiopia	Afghanistan	Niger
11	Haiti	Chad	Myanmar	Iran	Burundi
12	Guinea	Comoros	Guinea	Myanmar	Guinea
13	Nigeria	Tuvalu	Iraq	DRC	DRC
14	Zimbabwe	Zimbabwe	Niger	Turkmenistan	Ethiopia
15	Ethiopia	Haiti	Nigeria	Uzbekistan	Guinea-Bissau
16	Guinea-Bissau	Gambia	Angola	Haiti	Liberia
17	Burundi	Kiribati	Côte d'Ivoire	Chad	Syria
18	Pakistan	Djibouti	Guinea-Bissau	Iraq	Burkina Faso
19	Eritrea	Solomon Islands	Zimbabwe	Ethiopia	Uganda
20	Niger	Togo	Burkina Faso	Congo	Nigeria
21	Côte d'Ivoire	DRC	Cameroon	Tajikistan	Haiti

(Continued)

Table 3.2 (Continued)

Rank	Fragile States Index 2017	Harmonized List FY 2017	State Fragility Index 2016	BTI 2016	CIFP Fragility Index 2016
22	Kenya	Papua New Guinea	Mali	Laos	Gambia
23	Libya	Burundi	Mauritania	Zimbabwe	Pakistan
24	Uganda	Myanmar	Pakistan	Pakistan	Cameroon
25	Myanmar	Liberia	Rwanda	Venezuela	Mozambique
26	Cameroon	Madagascar	Uganda	Cambodia	Iraq
27	Liberia	Sierra Leone	Eritrea	Cuba	Mauritania
28	Mauritania	Côte d'Ivoire	Gambia	Angola	Côte d'Ivoire
29	Congo	Mali	Syria	Cameroon	Djibouti
30	North Korea	Kosovo	Haiti	Saudi Arabia	Congo
31	Mali	**Territories**	Malawi	Belarus	Zimbabwe
32	Angola	West Bank and Gaza	Congo	Mauritania	Sierra Leone
33	Nepal	**IBRD Only**	Liberia	Burundi	Comoros
34	Rwanda	Iraq	Libya	Egypt	Togo
35	Timor-Leste	Lebanon	Sierra Leone	Azerbaijan	Angola
36	Egypt	Libya	Togo	Morocco	West Bank and Gaza
37	Gambia	Syria	Bangladesh	Togo	Kenya
38	Sierra Leone		Djibouti	Burkina Faso	Tanzania
39	Bangladesh		Egypt	Vietnam	Myanmar
40	Mozambique		Equatorial Guinea	Nepal	Equatorial Guinea
			Kyrgyzstan		
			Laos		
			Philippines		
			Zambia		

Table 3.3 Unique countries: countries included in "most fragile 40" only on one list below

Fragile States Index 2017	Harmonized List FY 2017	State Fragility Index 2016	BTI 2016	CIFP Fragility Index 2016
Timor-Leste	Kiribati	Kyrgyzstan	Azerbaijan	Tanzania
	Kosovo	Malawi	Belarus	
	Lebanon	Philippines	Cambodia	
	Madagascar	Zambia	Cuba	
	Marshall Islands		Iran	
	Micronesia		Morocco	
	Papua New Guinea		Saudi Arabia	
	Solomon Islands		Tadjikistan	
	Tuvalu		Turkmenistan	
			Uzbekistan	
			Venezuela	
			Vietnam	

Table 3.4 Missing countries: countries included on more than one comparison list, but excluded from the lists below

Fragile States Index 2017	Harmonized List FY 2017	State Fragility Index 2015	BTI 2016	CIFP Fragility Index 2015
On four other lists				
	Angola			
	Cameroon			
	Congo			
			Côte d'Ivoire	
	Ethiopia			
			Gambia	
			Guinea-Bissau	
			Liberia	
				Libya
	Mauritania			
			Mali	
	Pakistan			
			Sierra Leone	
Togo				
On three other lists				
Djibouti			Djibouti	
	Egypt			Egypt
	Guinea		Guinea	
	Niger		Niger	
	Nigeria		Nigeria	
	Uganda		Uganda	

(Continued)

Table 3.4 (Continued)

Fragile States Index 2017	Harmonized List FY 2017	State Fragility Index 2015	BTI 2016	CIFP Fragility Index 2015
On two other lists				
	Bangladesh		Bangladesh	Bangladesh
Burkina Faso	Burkina Faso			Burkina Faso
Comoros		Comoros	Comoros	
Equatorial Guinea	Equatorial Guinea		Equatorial Guinea	
	Kenya	Kenya	Kenya	
Laos	Laos			Laos
	Mozambique	Mozambique	Mozambique	
	Nepal	Nepal		Nepal
	North Korea	North Korea		North Korea
	Rwanda		Rwanda	Rwanda
West Bank and Gaza		West Bank and Gaza	West Bank and Gaza	

policymakers and development practitioners are supposed to do with the lists, scores, and rankings, because they do not provide any guide on how policies or practices should be tailored to each country's particular concerns (Milante and Woolcock 2017).

Therefore, this research avoids the assumption of an arbitrary trade-off between variables and the use of composite indexes and fragility rankings. Instead, it proposes a simpler way to measure fragility using relevant and simple indicators that are already being produced operationally and are freely available. Each indicator is assumed to represent overall performance in each dimension of human fragility and is not offset by the value of any other indicator. The indicators used to assess human fragility are outlined in Table 3.5.

As defined above, people are insecure when they are exposed to immediate physical threats to life or deprived of life-sustaining resources. In order to measure physical threats to life, this methodology first looks at violent deaths as measured by two indicators that reflect the direct outcome of physical threat: "battle-related deaths" and "homicide victims." To measure physical threats to life, it looks at displaced people, such as refugees and internally displaced persons (IDPs), who are forced to leave their homes or countries in order to escape violent conflict. To measure deprivation of life-sustaining resources, the study uses the "poverty headcount ratio at $1.90 a day (2011 PPP)."

The coverage of social protection systems and the prevalence of undernourishment are used to measure human vulnerability. Given that social protection constitutes investment in people to empower them to adjust to change,

Table 3.5 Indicators for measuring human fragility

Human Fragility: *Situation or place where people are insecure or vulnerable to becoming insecure*

Dimension	Sub-dimension/ operational definition	Measurement	Source
Human Security	Immediate physical threats to life	a. Violent deaths rate (battle-related deaths per 100,000 + homicides per 100,000)	UCDP, UNODC
		b. Displacement rate (number of refugees per 100,000 + IDPs per 100,000)	UNHCR, IDMC
	Deprivation of life-sustaining resources	a. Poverty headcount ratio at $1.90 a day (2011 PPP, % of population)	World Bank
Vulnerability	Capacity to respond to physical threats and deprivation	a. Coverage of social protection (% of population)	World Bank
		b. Prevalence of undernourishment (% of population)	World Bank

Sources: On population, see World Bank (2017); on number of conflict deaths, see UCDP (2017); on homicide rate, see UNODC (2018); on number of refugees, see UNHCR (2017); on number of IDPs, see IDMC (2017a); on poverty headcount, see World Bank (2018b); on coverage of social protection see World Bank (2018a); and on prevalence of undernourishment and food security, see World Bank (2018c). Displacement rate and violent deaths rate are calculated by the author based on the listed data.

this acts as an automatic social and economic stabilizer (ILO 2012). For this reason, this indicator can show the extent to which people fall into insecurity or make the transition to a more sustainable status after shocks. Similarly, reducing malnutrition is considered critical to strengthening household capacity for response, as well-nourished individuals are healthier and have greater physical reserves and hence are better able to cope with shocks (FAO 2014).

After collecting the relevant data, the study mapped countries across a distribution of human fragility. This chapter zooms in on Southeast Asia to identify not only the most fragile countries, but also the subnational regions where people are most in need of assistance but often neglected, unprotected, and left behind.

Mapping human fragility

For the purposes of the analysis, countries were categorized as being challenged by human insecurity if (a) the rate of violent deaths puts them in the top 25 percent of countries; (b) they were in the top 40 percent of sources of refugees or IDPs per capita; or (c) the rate of extreme poverty was in the top 25 percent of countries. Specifically, a country was considered insecure if the rate of violent deaths per 100,000 population was greater than 9.68 – the top quartile of global violent deaths in 2016; the number of refugee and IDPs was greater than 74.89 per 100,000 population – the upper two quintiles for this statistic; or the proportion of people living on less than US$1.90 per day was greater than 24.44 percent of the population – the top quartile of the poverty headcount ratio.

This yields a list of 102 countries where people are insecure (see Table 3.6), 88 of which have high levels of physical threat, 42 high levels of deprivation, and 28 both. Table 3.6 also disaggregates countries by source of insecurity. Of the 88 countries facing high levels of physical threat, 66 have high levels of displacement, 50 high numbers of violent deaths, and 28 high levels of both violent death and displacement. Among the 42 highly deprived countries, nine have high levels of displacement, five high numbers of violent deaths, and 14 high levels of both violent death and displacement.

Geographically, sub-Saharan Africa is the most insecure region across all dimensions of human security: 43 of the 102 countries designated insecure, 24 of the 66 countries with high levels of displacement, 21 of the 50 countries with high levels of violent death, and 35 of the 42 highly deprived countries were in sub-Saharan Africa. Of the 14 countries in which displacement, violence, and deprivation are concentrated, 11 are located in the region. All the insecure countries in Europe and Central Asia, and the Middle East and North Africa (MENA) have problems primarily linked to high levels of displacement. In Latin America and the Caribbean, the problems are linked to high levels of violent death.

Similarly, countries are considered vulnerable if (a) all forms of social protection cover less than 29.8 percent of the population, which puts them in the bottom two quintiles for this statistic; or (b) the prevalence of undernourishment is greater than 14.95 percent of the population, which puts them in the top quartile for the statistic.

Table 3.7 lists 70 vulnerable countries: 48 with low levels of social protection, 47 with high levels of undernourishment, and 25 with both. Once again, the countries in sub-Saharan Africa are the most vulnerable due to low levels of social protection and high levels of undernourishment, followed by those in the Asia and the Pacific region.

Table 3.6 Human fragility: countries where people are insecure

	High physical threats			High deprivation	Total
	High displacement	High displacement and high violence	High violence		
Asia and the Pacific	Bangladesh, Bhutan, Cambodia, Fiji, Laos, Mongolia, Myanmar, Nepal, Pakistan, Sri Lanka, Vietnam	*Afghanistan,* Philippines	*Papua New Guinea,* Tuvalu	Solomon Island, Timor-Leste	17 (4)
Middle East and North Africa	Djibouti, Iran, Lebanon, West Bank and Gaza	Iraq, Libya, *Syria,* Yemen			8 (1)
Sub-Saharan Africa	*Burundi,* Cameroon, *Ethiopia, Gambia, Guinea, Liberia, Niger, Rwanda, Senegal, Togo,* Zimbabwe	*Central African Rep., Chad, DRC, Congo, Côte d'Ivoire, Eritrea, Guinea-Bissau, Mali,* Mauritania, *Nigeria, Somalia, South Sudan,* Sudan	*Angola,* Botswana, Cabo Verde, *Lesotho,* Namibia, South Africa, *Swaziland, Uganda*	Benin, Burkina Faso, Equatorial Guinea, Kenya, Madagascar, Malawi, Mozambique, Sao Tome and Principe, Sierra Leone, Tanzania, Zambia	43 (35)

(Continued)

Table 3.6 (Continued)

	High physical threats		High violence	High deprivation	Total
	High displacement	High displacement and high violence			
Latin America and the Caribbean	Antigua and Barbuda, Grenada	Bahamas, Colombia, El Salvador, Guatemala, ***Haiti***, Honduras, St. Lucia, St. Kitts and Nevis, St. Vincent and the Grenadines	Belize, Brazil, Cayman Islands, Costa Rica, Dominican Rep., Guyana, Jamaica, Mexico, Panama, Puerto Rico, Trinidad and Tobago, Venezuela		23 (1)
Europe and Central Asia	Albania, Armenia, Azerbaijan, Bosnia and Herzegovina, Croatia, Georgia, Montenegro, Serbia, Turkey, Ukraine			Tajikistan	11 (1)
		88 (28)		(14)	
Total	38 (9)	28 (14)	22 (5)		102 (42)

Note: Countries in bold and italic have high levels of insecurity and deprivation. Figures in parentheses indicate the number of highly deprived countries.

Table 3.7 Human fragility: countries where people are vulnerable

	Low social protection	Low social protection and high undernourishment	High undernourishment	Total
Asia and the Pacific	Bhutan, Fiji, Kiribati, Maldives, Micronesia, Papua New Guinea, Solomon Islands, Tonga	Afghanistan, Bangladesh, Cambodia, Laos, Myanmar, Pakistan	Mongolia, North Korea, Sri Lanka, Timor-Leste	18
Middle East and North Africa	Djibouti, Tunisia, West Bank and Gaza	Syria, Yemen	Iraq	6
Sub-Saharan Africa	Benin, Cabo Verde, Cameroon, Comoros, DRC, Mali, Niger, Nigeria, Senegal, Togo	Burkina Faso, Central African Rep., Chad, Congo, Côte d'Ivoire, Ethiopia, Kenya, Madagascar, Mozambique, Namibia, Sierra Leone, South Sudan, Sudan, Tanzania, Zambia, Zimbabwe	Botswana, Burundi, Guinea, Guinea-Bissau, Liberia, Malawi, Rwanda, Somalia, Swaziland, Uganda	36
Latin America and the Caribbean	Dominica, Venezuela	Haiti	Antigua and Barbuda, Bolivia, Grenada, Guatemala, Nicaragua, St. Lucia	9
Europe and Central Asia			Tajikistan	1
Total	23	25	22	70

In sum, the 112 countries in Table 3.8 face high levels of human fragility: 60 face the challenges of both human insecurity and vulnerability, while 10 are not insecure but vulnerable to becoming insecure. More than half of the insecure countries (60 out of 102) are highly unlikely to recover from their insecure situations in the near future. One-third of the insecure or vulnerable countries (44 out of 112) are concentrated in sub-Saharan Africa. The

Table 3.8 Mapping human fragility at the cross-country level

	Human insecurity	Human insecurity and human vulnerability	Human vulnerability	Total
Asia and the Pacific	Nepal, Philippines, Tuvalu, Vietnam	Afghanistan, Bangladesh, Bhutan, Cambodia, Fiji, Laos, Mongolia, Myanmar, Pakistan, Papua New Guinea, Solomon Islands, Sri Lanka, Timor-Leste	Kiribati, Maldives, Micronesia, North Korea, Tonga	22
Middle East and North Africa	Iran, Lebanon, Libya	Djibouti, Iraq, Syria, West Bank and Gaza, Yemen	Tunisia	9
Sub-Saharan Africa	Angola, Equatorial Guinea, Eritrea, Gambia, Lesotho, Mauritania, Sao Tome and Principe, South Africa	Benin, Botswana, Burkina Faso, Burundi, Cabo Verde, Cameroon, Central African Rep., Chad, DRC, Congo, Côte d'Ivoire, Ethiopia, Guinea, Guinea-Bissau, Kenya, Liberia, Madagascar, Malawi, Mali, Mozambique, Namibia, Niger, Nigeria, Rwanda, Senegal, Sierra Leone, Somalia, South Sudan, Sudan, Swaziland, Tanzania, Togo, Uganda, Zambia, Zimbabwe	Comoros	44
Latin America and the Caribbean	Bahamas, Belize, Brazil, Cayman Islands, Colombia, Costa Rica, Dominican Rep., El Salvador, Guyana, Honduras, Jamaica, Mexico, Panama, Puerto Rico, St. Kitts and Nevis, St. Vincent and the Grenadines, Trinidad and Tobago	Antigua and Barbuda, Grenada, Guatemala, Haiti, St. Lucia, Venezuela	Bolivia, Dominica, Nicaragua	26
Europe and Central Asia	Albania, Armenia, Azerbaijan, Bosnia and Herzegovina, Croatia, Georgia, Montenegro, Serbia, Turkey, Ukraine	Tajikistan		11
Total	42	60	10	112

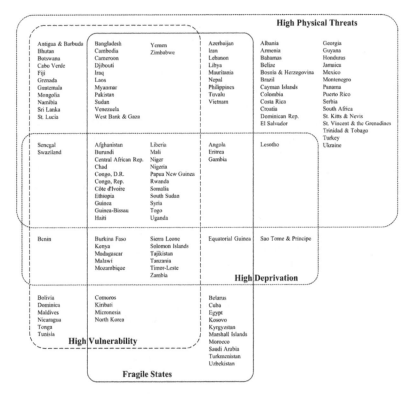

Figure 3.2 Human fragility vs. state fragility

only vulnerable country in the Europe and Central Asia region, Tajikistan, is categorized as insecure because of its high levels of deprivation.

For further comparison, Figure 3.2 shows human fragility overlaid with the combined list of fragile states from the five most widely used measurements of state fragility. There is clearly a significant overlap of countries where the four groupings intersect: 22 countries. In these countries there is little doubt about the presence or threat of violence and deprivation, and the concomitant fragility of their systems. Furthermore, approximately 85 percent of the combined fragile states list is captured by the human fragility designation. The fragile states not captured by the human fragility list are Belarus, Cuba, Egypt, Kosovo, Kyrgyzstan, Marshall Islands, Morocco, Saudi Arabia, Turkmenistan, and Uzbekistan.

Human fragility in Southeast Asia

The cross-country level analysis in the previous section can be complemented by scrutinizing human fragility at the subnational level, given that most of the places confronting human fragility are localities or subnational entities rather than states. For example, refugees and IDPs generally come from areas affected by conflict, and the rate of violent death can vary widely within countries. While the debate about the usefulness of designating countries as fragile through fragile states lists will continue, the mapping analysis in this section uses the designation "human fragility" to assess who is most vulnerable to being left behind at the regional and subnational levels, with a specific focus on Southeast Asia.

Of the 112 countries considered fragile, six are located in Southeast Asia: the CLMV (Cambodia, Laos, Myanmar, Vietnam) countries, the Philippines, and Timor-Leste. These six countries constitute roughly half the region's population and only 4 percent of the world's population, but the average of their indicators for violent deaths, refugees, displacement, and poverty is significantly higher than both the rest of the region and the global average. Table 3.9 provides some basic descriptive and comparative statistics on the countries.

Table 3.9 Descriptive statistics: countries where people are fragile in Southeast Asia, China, India, and the rest of the world, 2016

	Number of countries	*Total population (million)*	*Refugees*	*IDPs*	*Violent deaths*	*Poverty headcount*
			(thousand)		*(per 100,000 pop.)*	
Human Fragility	112	2,620	16,491	37,146	15.33	24.5
Southeast Asia	6	297.1	840	731	4.55	12.1
Cambodia	1	15.7	12.4	0	1.8	2.2
Laos	1	6.7	7.2	0	7.3	22.7
Myanmar	1	52.8	490.3	644	2.7	6.5
Philippines	1	103.3	0.42	87.4	10.3	8.3
Timor-Leste	1	1.3	0.01	0	3.7	30.3
Vietnam	1	92.7	329.3	0	1.5	2.8
China	1	1,378	207	0	0.8	1.8
India	1	1,324	7.2	0	1.5	21.2
Rest of the World	98	2,087	157.9	35	2.97	1.92
Rest of Southeast Asia	5	342.3	13	0	1.43	2.3

Note: Due to their scale, China and India are considered separately in this analysis.

Given that all these states are already regarded as highly fragile according to the five measurements of state fragility examined above (see Table 3.2), the designation "human fragility" certainly captures the core of the "most fragile" situations in the region, by any definition. In addition, the human fragility designation picks up countries for which violence or the threat of violence are clearly affecting development, either directly through conflict or the displacement of those fleeing dangerous places to escape persecution or seek greater freedom, or through deprivation.

First and foremost, the CLMV countries and the Philippines are the major sources of displacement in the region. Myanmar, in particular, is host to around 1 million stateless people, mostly Rohingya minorities.[6] The majority live in northern Rakhine State, which shares a border with Bangladesh. This is the greatest scale of displacement in the region in terms of the number of refugees per host country population, as well as the largest concentration of stateless persons worldwide. In addition to the stateless, an additional 644,000 IDPs are dispersed mainly across Rakhine State (120,000), Kachin, and northern Shan states (97,000), which border China, and parts of the southeast of Myanmar (400,000) near the border with Thailand. Furthermore, 490,000 Rohingya refugees are dispersed in neighboring countries, mostly in the Cox's Bazar District of Bangladesh (276,198), on the Thailand-Myanmar border (102,663), and in Malaysia (87,036).[7]

Protracted displacement linked to a long history of conflict can also be found in the Philippines. The Philippines is the only Southeast Asian country that is currently experiencing high levels of both displacement and violent deaths. However, most of the violent and armed conflicts that cause displacement and casualties are concentrated in the Mindanao region. As of 2016, 87,000 people had been displaced by conflict in the Mindanao region, most (81,000) in the Autonomous Region in Muslim Mindanao (ARRM), 28,616 of whom were displaced before 2014 (IDMC 2017b). While 280,000 people had been newly displaced by conflict and violence in 2016, most have since returned to their homes even though the conflict is continuing. The relatively high return rate of the displaced population in the conflict-affected areas of Mindanao means that people are being regularly displaced by the prolonged armed violence and such multiple displacements and regular returns have become common in the region.

Cambodia and Vietnam are captured in only one of the five indexes (see Table 3.3). Their inclusion should raise questions about why the number of displaced persons from these countries exceeds 74.89 per 100,000 population. Furthermore, although the region in general has shown gradual progress in socioeconomic development and poverty reduction, the challenges posed by conflict and fragility persist. For example, in the Philippines, subnational conflicts have intensified even as growth has accelerated. Similarly, rapid economic expansion in Cambodia has contributed to resource conflict by reducing the security of land tenure for many (Asia Foundation 2017, 3). It is frequently argued that increased levels of economic development will eventually reduce the frequency and severity of violent conflict (Collier 2000; Gorman 2011). While there may be evidence for this in other cases or regions, the evidence from Southeast Asia is that development does not necessarily guarantee or bring about peace and a combination of other factors should be considered (Homer-Dixon 1994; Mac Ginty and Williams 2016; Sen 2006). The results of the analysis of human fragility in Southeast Asia thus reveal the need for specific development and/or humanitarian programs.

Conclusion

This chapter builds on the premise that it is crucial to deepen our understanding of countries where development lags, referred to as fragile states, and to broaden our view of which solutions promote positive change in such places. In this regard, a human fragility framework is proposed to enable fragility analysis that complements the current state-centered approach to fragility.

A human fragility framework identifies the different drivers of fragility, which allows better matching of fragile countries by typology. For example, while all the designated Southeast Asian countries are deemed fragile in terms of human security, the CLMV countries and the Philippines are insecure because of their high levels of displacement. Timor-Leste also faces human insecurity, but this is due to the high level of violent deaths. A human fragility approach can help to inform better targeted responses.

Even in countries categorized as challenged by human fragility, certain subnational locations, such as northern Rakhine State in Myanmar, Mindanao in the Philippines, or the border areas of a region, will be more fragile than others, depending on the concentrations of insecure or vulnerable people. Given that displacement tends to spill over into places that are already experiencing human fragility, insecure people displaced by conflict and violence are more likely to be unsafe and caught up in a protracted displacement, thereby causing further vulnerability and a vicious cycle of human fragility.

Nonetheless, it would be incorrect to assume that the presence of conditions of insecurity or vulnerability is the problem in itself. Instead, the problem is the ways in which such conditions are experienced, and the circumstances under which such conditions tend to put people at risk of becoming poor, insecure, and vulnerable. It will therefore be necessary to undertake further research into how and why relevant institutions – not necessarily states – are unable to deal successfully with human fragility. This would help to identify the places where development and/or humanitarian assistance, and state policies either do not or cannot reach people, thereby allowing them to lag behind. Policymakers could then make better-informed decisions about which forms of practice or assistance are most needed and supportable.

Notes

1 The research for this chapter was supported by the Policy-Oriented Research Grant Program through the Korea Foundation. The chapter is based on the author's doctoral thesis.
2 Some highlight the vagueness of the concept and associated problems of measurement or definition (Anderson 1996; Maass and Mepham 2004; OECD DAC 1997, 1998, 2001). Others criticize it for being a new form of Western control (Khong 2001, 232; Krause 2004, 367; Martin and Owen 2010; Newman 2010, 82; Paris 2001, 88). Still others see the danger that a division between the haves and the have nots might disempower the latter (Duffield 2007; Suhrke 1999).
3 The Harmonized List uses harmonized average scores to rank the countries.
4 These are Afghanistan, the Central African Republic, Somalia, South Sudan, Sudan, and Yemen.
5 These countries are Afghanistan, Burundi, the Central African Republic, Chad, the Democratic Republic of the Congo, Eritrea, Haiti, Iraq, Myanmar, Somalia, South Sudan, Sudan, Syria, Yemen, and Zimbabwe.
6 The Rohingya is an ethnic, religious (Muslim), and linguistic minority that has been deprived of its rights to nationality and citizenship by the Myanmar government.
7 Tensions between the Buddhist and Muslim communities in Rakhine State escalated dramatically after August 2017. The number of Rohingya refugees had increased to 869,994, as of March 2018.

References

Adalbert Hampel, K. (2015) "The dark(er) side of 'state failure': Sate formation and socio-political variation" *Third World Quarterly* 36(9) 1629–48.

Adger, W. N. (2006) "Vulnerability" *Global Environmental Change* 16(3) 268–81.

Agamben, G. (2005) *State of Exception* University of Chicago Press, Chicago.

Alexander, M., Willman, A., Aslam, G., Rebosio, M., and Balasuriya, K. (2013) *Societal Dynamics and Fragility* World Bank, Washington, DC.

Anderson, M. B. (1996) *Do No Harm: Supporting Local Capacities for Peace through Aid* Local Capacities for Peace Project, Cambridge.

Asia Foundation (2017) *The State of Conflict and Violence in Asia* The Asia Foundation, Bangkok.

Berkes, F. (2007) "Understanding uncertainty and reducing vulnerability: Lessons from resilience thinking" *Natural Hazards* 41(2) 283–95.

Bertelsmann Stiftung (2016) *Transformation Index, BTI 2016: Political Management in International Comparison* Verlag Bertelsmann Stiftung, Gütersloh.

Bertoli, S. and Ticci, E. (2012) "A fragile guideline to development assistance" *Development Policy Review* 30(2) 211–30.

Bøås, M. and Jennings, K. M. (2005) "Insecurity and development: The rhetoric of the 'failed state'" *European Journal of Development Research* 17(3) 385–95.

Boege, V., Brown, M. A., and Clements, K. P. (2009) "Hybrid political orders, not fragile states" *Peace Review* 21(1) 13–21.

Boyd, E., Osbahr, H., Ericksen, P. J., Tompkins, E. L., Lemos, M. C., and Miller, F. (2008) "Resilience and 'climatizing' development: Examples and policy implications" *Development* 51(3) 390–96.

Branchflower, A. (2004) "How important are difficult environments to achieving the MDGs?" *Poverty Reduction in Difficult Environments (PRDE) Working Paper No. 2* DFID, London.

Brinkerhoff, D. W. (2011) "State fragility and governance: Conflict mitigation and subnational perspective" *Development Policy Review* 29(2) 131–53.

Cammack, D., McLeod, D., Menocal, A. R., and Christiansen, K. (2006) *Donors and the "Fragile States" Agenda: A Survey of Current Thinking and Practice* Overseas Development Institute, London.

Cannon, T. (2008) *Reducing People's Vulnerability to Natural Hazards* UN University World Institute for Development Economics Research, Helsinki.

Carment, D., Prest, S., and Samy, Y. (2010) *Security, Development, and the Fragile State: Bridging the Gap between Theory and Policy* Routledge, New York.

Carment, D., Tikuisis, P., Samy, Y., and Floch, J. (2017) *The CIFP Fragility Index: New Trends and Categorizations* Country Indicators for Foreign Policy, Ottawa.

Collier, P. (2000) *Economic Causes of Civil Conflict and Their Implications for Policy* World Bank, Washington, DC.

Country Indicators for Foreign Policy (CIFP) (2006) *Failed and Fragile States: A Concept Paper for the Canadian Government* CIFP, Ottawa.

de Boer, J. (2015) "Resilience and the fragile city" *Stability: International Journal of Security & Development* 4(1) 1–7.

Department for International Development (DFID) (2005) *Why We Need to Work More Effectively in Fragile States* DFID, London.

Duffield, M. (2007) *Development, Security and Unending War: Governing the World of Peoples* Policy Press, Cambridge.

Food and Agriculture Organization of the United Nations (FAO) (2014) *Nutrition and Resilience: Strengthening the Links between Resilience and Nutrition in Food and Agriculture* FAO, Rome.

Fukuyama, F. (2004) *State-Building: Governance and World Order in the 21st Century* Cornell University Press, New York.

Gallopín, G. C. (2006) "Linkages between vulnerability, resilience, and adaptive capacity" *Global Environmental Change* 16(3) 293–303.

Gates, R. M. (2010) Helping others defend themselves: The future of US security assistance *Foreign Affairs* May/June (www.foreignaffairs.com/articles/2010-05-01/helping-others-defend-themselves) Accessed July 11, 2018.

Gorman, E. (2011) *Conflict and Development* Zed Books, New York.

Graham, S. (2010) *Cities under Siege: The New Military Urbanism* Verso, London and New York.

Guo, R. and Freeman, C. eds. (2011) *Managing Fragile Regions: Method and Application* Springer, New York.

Gutiérrez Sanín, F. (2009) *The Quandaries of Coding and Ranking: Evaluating Poor State Performance Indexes* London School of Economics and Political Science, London.

—— (2011) "Evaluating state performance: A critical view of state failure and fragility indexes" *European Journal of Development Research* 23(1) 20–42.

Homer-Dixon, T. (1994) "Environmental scarcities and violent conflict: Evidence from cases" *International Security* 19(1) 5–40.

Ignatieff, M. (2002) "Intervention and state failure" *Dissent* 49(1) 1945–91.

Internal Displacement Monitoring Center (IDMC) (2017a) *Global Report on Internal Displacement 2017* IDMC, Geneva.

—— (2017b) "Philippines: Displacement context" (www.internal-displacement. org/countries/philippines) Accessed April 6, 2018.

International Development Research Centre (ICISS) (2001) *The Responsibility to Protect* ICISS, Ottawa.

International Labour Organization (ILO) (2012) "Social protection floors recommendation no. 202" (www.ilo.org/dyn/normlex/en/f?p=NORMLEXPUB:12100: 0::NO::P12100_ILO_CODE:R202) Accessed February 8, 2018.

Jang, S. and Milante, G. (2016) "9-I: Development in dangerous places" in *SIPRI Yearbook 2016: Armaments, Disarmament and International Security* Oxford University Press, Oxford.

Jensen, S. (2010) "The security and development nexus in Cape Town: War on gangs, counterinsurgency and citizenship" *Security Dialogue* 41(1) 77–98.

Kaplan, S. D. (2010) "Rethinking state-building in a failed state" *The Washington Quarterly* 33(1) 81–97.

Kasperson, R. E., Dow, K., Archer, E., Caceres, D., Downing, T., Elmqvist, T., Eriksen, S., Folke, C., Han, G., Iyengar, K., Vogel, C., Wilson, K., and Ziervogel, G. (2005) "Vulnerable people and places" in Hassan, R., Sholes, R. and Ash, N. eds., *Ecosystems and Human Wellbeing: Current State and Trends* Volume 1 Island Press, Washington, DC.

Khong, Y. F. (2001) "Human security: A shotgun approach to alleviating human misery?" *Global Governance* 7(3) 231–6.

King, G. and Christopher, M. (2001) "Rethinking human security" *Political Science Quarterly* 116(4) 585–610.

Krause, K. (2004) "The key to a powerful agenda, if properly defined" *Security Dialogue* 35(3) 367–8.

Leander, A. (2009) *Signposting Four Pitfalls: A Reflection on Historical Sociology and IR* Department of Intercultural Communication and Management, Copenhagen Business School, Frederiksberg, Copenhagen.

Lederach, J. P. (1997) *Building Peace* United States Institute of Peace, Washington, DC.

—— (1999) *The Journey toward Reconciliation* Herald Press, Scottdale.

Lucchi, E. (2013) *Humanitarian Interventions in Situations of Urban Violence* Active Learning Network for Accountability and Performance/Overseas Development Institute, London.

Maass, G. and Mepham, D. (2004) *Promoting Effective States: A Progressive Policy Response to Failed and Failing States* Institute for Public Policy Research and Friedrich-Ebert-Stiftung, London.

Mac Ginty, R. and Williams, A. (2016) *Conflict and Development* Routledge, Oxon.

Madrueño-Aguilar, R. (2016) "Human security and the new global threats: Discourse, taxonomy and implications" *Global Policy* 7(2) 156–73.

Marshall, M. G. and Elzinga-Marshall, G. (2017) *Global Report 2017: Conflict, Governance, and State Fragility* Center for Systemic Peace, Vienna, VA.

Martin, M. and Owen, T. (2010) "The second generation of human security: Lessons from the un and EU experience" *International Affairs* 86(1) 211–24.

Messner, J. J., Haken, N., Blyth, H., Murphy, C., Quinn, A., Lehner, G., and Ganz, D. (2017) *Fragile States Index, 2017: Annual Report* Fund for Peace, Washington, DC.

Milante, G. (2017) "6-I: Peace and development" *SIPRI Yearbook 2017: Armaments, Disarmament and International Security* Oxford University Press, Oxford.

Milante, G. and Woolcock, M. (2017) "New approaches to identifying state fragility" *Journal of Globalization and Development* 8(1) 1–10.

Miller, F., Osbahr, H., Boyd, E., Thomalla, F., Bharwani, S., Ziervogel, G., Walker, B., Birkmann, J., van der Leeuw, S., Rockström, J., Hinkel, J., Downing, T., Folke, C., and Nelson, D. (2010) "Resilience and vulnerability: Complementary or conflicting concepts?" *Ecology and Society* 15(3).

Mitchell, T. (1991) "The limits of the state: Beyond statist approaches and their critics" *American Political Science Review* 85(1) 77–96.

Muggah, R. (2013) "Fragile cities rising" *IPI Global Observatory* July 10 (https://theglobalobservatory.org/2013/07/fragile-cities-rising/) Accessed July 11, 2018.

Muggah, R. and Savage, K. (2012) "Urban violence and humanitarian action: Engaging the fragile city" *Journal of Humanitarian Assistance*.

Naudé, W., McGillivray, M., and Rossow, S. (2009) "Measuring the vulnerability of subnational regions in South Africa" *Oxford Development Studies* 37(3) 249–76.

Nelson, D. R., Adger, W. N., and Brown, K. (2007) "Adaptation to environmental change: Contributions of a resilience framework" *Annual Review of Environment and Resources* 32(1) 395–419.

Newman, E. (2010) "Critical human security studies" *Review of International Studies* 36(1) 77–94.

Nogueira, J. P. (2017) "From failed states to fragile cities: Redefining spaces of humanitarian practice" *Third World Quarterly* 38(7) 1437–53.

Nuscheler, F., Debiel, T., and Messner, D. (2007) "Global vulnerabilities and threats to 'human security'" in Debiel, T., Messner, D. and Nuscheler, F. eds., *Global Trends 2007: Vulnerability and Human Security in the 21st Century* Development and Peace Foundation, Bonn.

Organisation for Economic Co-Operation and Development (OECD) (2007) *Principles for Good International Engagement in Fragile States and Situations* OECD, Paris.

Organisation for Economic Co-Operation and Development Development Co-Operation Directorate (OECD DAC) (1997) *DAC Guidelines on Conflict, Peace and Development Co-Operation* OECD, Paris.

──── (1998) *Conflict, Peace and Development Co-Operation on the Threshold of the 21st Century* OECD, Paris.

──── (2001) *Helping Prevent Violent Conflict* OECD, Paris.

Orjuela, C. (2010) "The bullet in the living room: Linking security and development in Colombo neighbourhood" *Security Dialogue* 41(1) 99–120.

Osbahr, H., Twyman, C., Neil Adger, W., and Thomas, D. S. G. (2008) "Effective livelihood adaptation to climate change disturbance: Scale dimensions of practice in Mozambique" *Geoforum* 39(6) 1951–64.

Paris, R. (2001) "Human security: Paradigm shift or hot air" *International Security* 26(2) 87–102.

Pouligny, B. (2010) *State-Society Relations and Intangible Dimensions of State Resilience and State Building: A Bottom-Up Perspective* European University Institute, Florence.

Sen, A. (2006) *Identity and Violence* Norton, New York.

Stedman, S. J. and Tanner, F. (2003) *Refugee Manipulation: War, Politics, and the Abuse of Human Suffering* Brookings Institution, Washington, DC.

Stern, M. and Öjendal, J. (2010) "Mapping the security-development nexus: Conflict, complexity, cacophony, convergence?" *Security Dialogue* 41(1) 5–29.

Suhrke, A. (1999) "Human security and the interests of states" *Security Dialogue* 30(3) 265–75.

Taleb, N. N. (2012) *Antifragile: Things That Gain from Disorder* Random House, New York.

Thomas, D. S. G., Twyman, C., Osbahr, H., and Hewitson, B. (2007) "Adaptation to climate change and variability: Farmer responses to intra-seasonal precipitation trends in South Africa" *Climatic Change* 83(3) 301–22.

United Nations (UN) (2004) *A More Secure World: Our Shared Responsibility, Report of the High-Level Panel on Threats, Challenges, and Change* United Nations, New York.

United Nations Development Programme (UNDP) (1994) *Human Development Report* Oxford University Press, Oxford.

United Nations High Commissioner for Refugees (UNHCR) (2017) *Global Trends: Forced Displacement in 2016* UNHCR, Geneva.

United Nations Office for the Coordination of Humanitarian Affairs (OCHA) (2009) *Human Security in Theory and Practice: Application of the Human Security Concept and the United Nations Trust Fund for Human Security* United Nations, New York.

United Nations Office on Drugs and Crime (UNODC) (2018) "UNODC statistics" (https://data.unodc.org/#state:0) Accessed May 23, 2018.

Uppsala Conflict Data Program (UCDP) (2017) "UCDP battle-related deaths dataset" (http://ucdp.uu.se/downloads/) Accessed May 21, 2018.

US Agency for International Development (USAID) (2005) *Fragile Sates Strategy* USAID, Washington, DC.

Walker, B., Holling, C. S., Carpenter, S. R., and Kinzig, A. P. (2004) "Resilience, adaptability and transformability in social-ecological systems" *Ecology and Society* 9(2).

Wisner, B., Blaikie, P., Cannon, T., and Davis, I. (2003) *At Risk: Natural Hazards, People's Vulnerability and Disasters* Routledge, London.

World Bank (2011) "From violence to resilience: Restoring confidence and trans-forming institutions" in *World Development Report 2011* World Bank, Washington, DC.

———— (2016) "Harmonized list of fragile situations, FY 17" (http://pubdocs.worldbank.org/en/154851467143896227/FY17HLFS-Final-6272016.pdf) Accessed May 18, 2018.

———— (2017) "Population, total" (https://data.worldbank.org/indicator/SP.POP.TOTL) Accessed May 18, 2018.

———— (2018a) "ASPIRE: The atlas of social protection indicators of resilience and equity" (http://datatopics.worldbank.org/aspire/) Accessed May 23, 2018.

———— (2018b) "DataBank: World development indicators" *Poverty Headcount Ratio at $1.90 a day (2011 PPP) (% of Population)* (http://databank.worldbank.org/data/reports.aspx?source=2&series=SI.POV.DDAY&country=) Accessed May 23, 2018.

———— (2018c) "DataBank: World development indicators" *Prevalence of under-nourishment (% of Population)* (http://databank.worldbank.org/data/reports.aspx?source=2&series=SN.ITK.DEFC.ZS&country=) Accessed May 23, 2018.

Ziaja, S. (2012) "What do fragility indices measure? Assessing measurement proce-dures and statistical proximity" *Zeitschrift für Vergleichende Politikwissenschaft* 6(1) 33–64.

Zoellick, R. B. (2008) "Fragile states: Securing development" *Survival* 50(6) 67–84.

Zou, L. and Thomalla, F. (2008) *The Causes of Social Vulnerability to Coastal Haz-ards in Southeast Asia* Stockholm Environment Institute, Stockholm.

4 Japanese contributions to peacebuilding, development, and human security in Southeast Asia

Ako Muto and Sachiko Ishikawa[1]

Introduction

Since the early 1990s, after the end of the Cold War, the international cooperation paradigm has generally shifted away from economic development
toward social and human development. This can particularly be seen in
the emergence of perspectives on development, peacebuilding, and human
security. Increasing numbers of intrastate conflicts required peacebuilding
aside from peacekeeping and peacemaking, as articulated by Boutros-Ghali
in 1992 (Boutros-Ghali 1992). Human security was another by-product of
globalization, which focused on a people-centered approach. To promote
such people-centered approaches, there was considerable discussion over
various issues such as poverty, gender, environment and governance, and
explorations of possible new and effective approaches.

With such drastic changes occurring in international society, Japan
shifted its focus to support the emerging concept of human security. Japan
had, in fact, struggled to find niches to contribute to addressing the global
consequences of globalization without mobilizing its military forces. The
country was seeking to regain its honored status – a goal stated in the Constitution of Japan – in the international community, especially after the
Gulf War of 1990–1991(Funabashi 1990). At the multilateral engagement
level, Japan took part positively in the UN arena to facilitate and concret-
ize the concept of human security. After more than a decade of discussions
and consultations, a UN General Assembly Resolution (A/RES/66/290) in
October 2012 adopted eight principles of human security and clarified the
concept of human security as distinct from the Responsibility to Protect
(R2P) (United Nations 2012). The international community finally con-
firmed the concept of human security, which relied on respect for the sovereignty of countries through close collaboration with multiple stakeholders
such as international and regional organizations and civil society – without
using military force.

Second, at the development cooperation level, the Japanese government integrated the concept of human security into its Official Development Assistance (ODA). Since the first ODA Medium-Term Policy of 1999, the perspective of human security occupied a fundamental position in Japan's ODA (MOFA 1999). The latest Development Cooperation Charter of 2015 has maintained the approach of its predecessors, stipulating that human security is the guiding principle of Japan's development cooperation (MOFA 2015). Peacebuilding has been placed as a priority issue under the umbrella of human security since the ODA Charter of 2003 (MOFA 2003). In this sense, development, peacebuilding, and human security are all in one basket of Japan's policy on international cooperation. On the practical front, Japan has two tools to pursue human security: the Grant Assistance for Grassroots and Human Security Projects (GGP) is in the good hands of the Ministry of Foreign Affairs, while the other tool is the Japan International Cooperation Agency (JICA), tasked with implementing development assistance from the perspective of human security.

In terms of the practice of human security in the context of development assistance, East Asia – and Southeast Asia in particular – have been the main target areas for Japan, since "Asia is a region that has a close relationship with Japan and high relevance to its security and prosperity" (MOFA 2003, 2015). Japan subsequently became the leading donor to some of the countries in Southeast Asia and contributed to the prosperity and stabilization in the region. While the provision of support to sub-Saharan Africa, the Middle East and North Africa has increased in recent years, the largest portion has continued to go to Southeast Asia in 2016, with a total amount of more than US$16 billion (MOFA 2017). Japan has also been expected to take part in tackling some negative impacts arising from globalization, such as trafficking in persons and intrastate conflicts, with its ODA. In its response to this, Japan sought two different approaches derived from needs of the people on the ground: bringing the regional collaboration mechanism forward to tackle interstate challenges and searching for solutions derived from within local contexts.

While Southeast Asia has experienced "miraculous" growth (World Bank 1993), there are still various threats to human security. Some of these can be seen in the statistics and indicators described as human fragility in this book. People can easily fall into fragility if appropriate protection is not provided. In Southeast Asia and East Asian countries – namely China, Japan, and South Korea – the state is still expected to protect its people (Camilleri 2000; Newman 2013). In its first Official Development Assistance Charter (ODA Charter), adopted in 1992, Japan focused its ODA priorities on basic human needs, human resource development and state building (MOFA 1992). Given that state fragility and human fragility are both different sides of the same coin, the practice of state building and that of human security can strengthen each other.

This chapter will firstly examine the contribution of the Japanese government to facilitating the concept of human security at both the multilateral engagement and development assistance levels. With regard to the latter, the synergetic interactions between policy and the practice will be highlighted. Secondly, two different case studies of Japan's assistance, both of which elaborate Japan's flexible approaches to human security practice in the context of development and peacebuilding, will be presented. The first case focuses on regional networking to tackle trafficking in persons in Southeast Asia. JICA's assistance in this field is unique – an issue that initially emerged from aspects of safe migration and organized crime has been tackled by development assistance with the concept of human security. The second case sought to settle an intrastate conflict in the Philippines. JICA's involvement in the peace process between the Philippine government and the Moro Islamic Liberation Front (MILF) (hereafter referred to "the Mindanao peace process") has been the most visible peacebuilding assistance of Japan in terms of budget, manpower, and duration of involvement. At the end of the chapter, some conclusions and lessons learned will be offered.

Japan's contributions in bringing forward human security to ODA

Background

It was rational for the Japanese government to employ the concept of human security, incorporating it into ODA as an attractive feature. Since the end of the Cold War, Japan has searched for ways to restore her position in the international community. In particular, Japan's secondary position in the Western alliance in the Gulf War in 1990–1991 woke the country up to the fact that cash diplomacy was not enough to satisfy international demands (Lincoln 1993, 201). The hard lesson was that the international environment in the 1990s would no longer allow Japan to follow the same one-dimensional economic strategy that it had pursued for the previous 40 years (Edström 2009, 68). The limited role Japan took in the peacekeeping operations in Cambodia in 1992 also required the Japanese government to find an alternative means of international cooperation outside the sphere of military operations. It was inevitably understood that the constraints of military operations could be overcome by ODA (Tadokoro 1997, 270).

The ODA Charter adopted in 1992 showed the modification of Japan's ODA policies from absolute nonintervention principles to adopting more Western norms by examining the records of recipient countries on military spending, democracy, moves toward market economy, and human rights as conditions for granting assistance (Edström 2009, 148). This was part of Japan's efforts not to accept the risk of isolation from the donor community – although, in practice, Japan continued to take sensitive approaches to recipient countries so as not to jeopardize good relationships. In fact, Japan provided the largest amount of ODA (almost US$9 billion) in the world for the first time in 1989 and maintained this position until 2001 when the US returned as the top donor (MOFA 2004). Yasumoto observed that Japan's rise to "great power" was linked to its ODA policies and its ODA was recognized as Japan's first genuine step toward accepting the kind of international responsibilities required of greatness (Yasumoto 1995, 4).

Toward the end of the 1990s, after Japan's ODA budget disbursement had declined, along with the falling economic growth of the country, the Japanese government sought a new policy for its ODA, both for its own domestic taxpayers and for the international community. The concept of human security was the one that seemed best-suited to Japan's needs (Dan 2000, 326). In other words, in the prevailing situation where the austere financing situation made it hard to avoid reductions in the ODA budget, cuts in this key instrument of foreign policy could be compensated by the input of fresh ideas that human security embodied (Tanaka 2002). Japan has become one of the leading countries in facilitating the concept of human security through its ODA since the late 1990s in fulfilling its international responsibilities. The following two sub-sections will examine how Japan was involved in facilitating and consolidating the concept of human security, both in the international community and in its development assistance.

Facilitating human security at the multilateral engagement level

The Japanese government took part positively in the UN arena in helping to spread the concept of human security among the international community. It was consistent in its pursuit of a definition of human security and underlying principles until the international community made a clear distinction between human security and R2P. It was important for Japan to propel the international community toward recognizing human security as a new global norm to cope with negative by-products emerging from globalization. Human security was also expected to be the key concept for the resurgence of the country's status in the international community. As the human security concept was directly linked with ODA in the discourse of the Japanese government, it was also indispensable to define the concept of human security as distinct from R2P, and to make sure that the two principles – the respect of sovereignty in collaboration with multiple stakeholders and the use of no military force – could be clarified and become accepted.

There were three main institutional measures in the UN arena that the Japanese government strongly supported. These were the UN Trust Fund for Human Security (UNTFHS) as a tool for implementation; the Commission on Human Security to scrutinize the concept; and the Friends of Human Security as a forum in which pro-human security countries could participate. These measures finally led to the adoption of a resolution on human security in the UN General Assembly. First, in 1999, the UNTFHS for UN agencies was established to implement human security, although, initially, the UNTFHS had no conceptual framework available (Edström 2009, 159). The UNTFHS was gradually regarded as the main avenue by which the Japanese government translated human-security-related ideas into practice (Fukushima 2003, 148). Although Japan's initial contribution was the rather small amount of 500 million yen in 1999, its accumulated contributions had reached a total of 45.3 billion yen, spread across 238 projects, by the end of 2016 (MOFA 2017).

Second, following the establishment of the UNTFHS, there were urgent demands to deepen the understanding of human security among UN member countries. Following the establishment of the Human Security Network (HSN) in 1999 and the launch of the International Commission on Intervention and State Sovereignty (ICISS) in 2000, it became necessary to define human security as separate from the concept defined by the ICISS. In fact, the debate on human security in the ICISS concentrated on the concept of freedom from fear, which was subsequently determined to be the concept underlying R2P. Thus, the Commission on Human Security was established in 2001, with the support of Kofi Annan, the UN Secretary-General, under the direction of two chairpersons, Sadako Ogata and Amartya Sen. The final report, entitled *Human Security Now*, was submitted by the Commission to the UN Secretary-General in 2003. The report defined the concept of human security by paying attention to both freedom from want and freedom from fear. The significance of the report was to show the links between peace and development (Commission on Human Security 2003).

Third, the concept of human security was promoted among UN member countries for official adoption. The term "human security" first appeared in a resolution of the General Assembly in September 2005 (United Nations 2005). This was known as paragraph 143, which stated that UN member countries would commit themselves to discussing and defining the notion of human security in the General Assembly (United Nations 2005). Japan regarded paragraph 143 as one of the more successful results of its endeavors to promote human security in the UN arena (Kitaoka 2007, 59). In addition, Japan took part in organizing the Friends of Human Security Forum in 2006 to follow up on paragraph 143 and to further enhance common understandings of human security, which was generally in line with the definition provided by the Commission on Human Security (MOFA 2006). By the last meeting in December 2009, the Forum had been held seven times (MOFA 2016). Ambassador Yukio Takasu, as co-chair of the meeting, proposed that the Friends of Human Security Forum should continue to focus on the application of the human security concept for UN activities and the mainstreaming of the concept in its policy framework (MOFA 2007).

All these series of discussions helped formed the basis for the UN General Assembly resolution titled "Follow-Up to Paragraph 143 on Human Security of the 2005 World Summit Outcome (A/RES/66/290)" in October 2012 (United Nations 2012). It has now been officially recognized that human security is distinct from R2P and its implementation. Absence of military operations and respect for the sovereignty of a country in collaboration with multiple stakeholders were clearly defined as the core principles for human security. Following the UN resolution, Japan increased its support for human security in the UN. The UNTFHS has continuously provided funds for human security programs of UN agencies. Ambassador Yukio Takasu has also been playing a role as Special Advisor to the UN Secretary-General on human security since 2010.

Consolidation of human security at the development assistance level

While peace and development have been linked with the concept of human security in the UN, the Japanese government has also accelerated to streamline the concept of human security in its development assistance policy. The significance in streamlining and strengthening human security in ODA policies is to enhance the synergetic effects between policymakers and practitioners – more precisely MOFA and JICA. From the policymakers' side, human security appeared for the first time as one of the basic approaches of Japan's ODA in the Medium-Term ODA Policy of 1999 (MOFA 1999). In the revised ODA Charter of 2003, human security was promoted as a basic policy, and peacebuilding was a priority issue under the umbrella of human security (MOFA 2003). It was understood that conflict prevention through poverty reduction and the correction of disparities was the prime role for Japan's ODA as peacebuilding, which was followed by "assistance to expedite the ending of the conflict and assistance for the consolidation of peace and nation-building in post-conflict situations" (MOFA 2003).

From the practitioners' side, Sadako Ogata was appointed as president of JICA in the same year that she completed her role as co-chair of the Commission on Human Security. She was expected to implement human security in ODA (Edström 2011, 45). Since then, her idealism and activism have wielded a profound and lasting influence on JICA's organizational culture (Kamidohzono, Gómez, and Mine 2016). Human security became one of the three pillars of the organization's reform in the larger context of administrative reform in Japan. Aside from the strong initiative from the top, "there was also a bottom-up attempt by JICA practitioners to identify the best way to reflect the human security idea in their operations" (Kamidohzono, Gómez, and Mine 2016, 208). After internal discussions, seven perspectives on human security were shared among JICA staff members in June 2004. These were subsequently modified to become four perspectives and four approaches, which became core principles for ODA implementation among JICA practitioners. Some synergetic effects were noticed when the ODA Medium-Term Policy was announced in 2005. As Kamidohzono et al. discussed, most of the four perspectives and four approaches were shared in Japan's Medium-Term ODA Policy (Kamidohzono, Gómez, and Mine 2016).

Through all these efforts, human security and peacebuilding have been retained as a basic policy and a priority issue respectively in the newly introduced Development Cooperation Charter of 2015. It can thus be concluded that JICA's practical views have clarified and strengthened Japan's ODA policies over the last 15 years. The whole structure of Japan's contribution to human security in three aspects is illustrated in Figure 4.1. On the

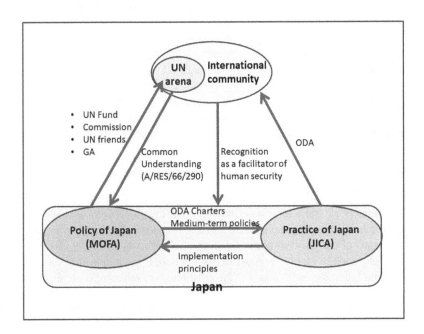

Figure 4.1 Japan's advocacy of human security

other hand, it has to be recognized that "the Japanese government and even JICA understood human security mainly as a foreign policy guideline, not as something applicable to its domestic issues" until Great East Japan Earthquake in 2011 and subsequent radioactive contamination in Fukushima prefecture (Kurusu 2016, 24). The devastation gave them an idea of downside risks in Japan and the necessity of applying the human security concept to domestic issues. The following two sections will examine how practices of human security vary on the ground, sometimes leading to new ways of implementing "top-down" and "bottom-up" approaches and of supporting regional networking, playing the role of catalyst and extending the approach beyond initial expectations.

Human security in practice 1: combatting trafficking in persons in Southeast Asia

While globalization has allowed people to move more dynamically across borders, there are also aspects of this that could be considered negative outcomes of globalization. Some of the people who cross borders do so as a result of human security threats: refugees, asylum seekers, smugglers, trafficked persons, and so on. Among these groups, trafficked persons might be considered one of the most vulnerable as they were trafficked without their knowledge or permission and are exploited only for the benefit of the traffickers. Japan, as a participant in global and regional frameworks against trafficking in persons, conducts bilateral technical cooperation projects in Thailand, Myanmar, and Vietnam through JICA. This section elaborates how Japan's bilateral cooperation has contributed to expanding regional networking among stakeholders in Southeast Asia with the goal of combatting trafficking in persons and discusses some key elements of Japan's technical cooperation projects in regard to human security.

Nexus among trafficking in persons, human security, development, and peacebuilding

The concept of "trafficking in persons" refers to the process and the condition of "the recruitment, transportation, transfer, harboring, or receipt of persons, by means of the threat or use of force or other forms of coercion, of abduction, of fraud [. . .] for the purpose of exploitation. Exploitation shall include, at a minimum, the exploitation of the prostitution of others or other forms of sexual exploitation, -forced labor or services, slavery or practices similar to slavery, servitude, or the removal of organs" (United Nations 2000).

The victims themselves are often treated as criminals: some are considered to be smugglers because they have crossed the border illegally, although they were deceived by traffickers; others are considered as illegal residents because traffickers often take their passports away and do not undertake the procedures necessary to obtain visas. Such people may be deported to their home countries as criminals. The victims can also face serious threats twice, both during exploitation and after being rescued. From a human security perspective, a victim-centered approach should be a higher priority than a criminal law response (Okubo and Shelley 2011, 2).

The research on trafficking in persons has been explored from the perspective of the multidisciplinary fields of migration studies, globalization, international relations, global business and industry, human rights, gender studies, legal studies, as well as security studies – particularly in the context of illegal migration and organized crime (Jonsson 2009, 1; Beeks and Amir 2006, xii). This research shows that trafficking in persons occurs for a range of different reasons. People become vulnerable through threats such as natural disasters, poverty, chronic unemployment, armed conflict, or through discrimination and marginalization based on intellectual or physical disability, gender, ethnicity, or other factors (United States Department of State 2002, 1; United States Department of State 2016, 8). Economic disparities may attract traffickers who entice the poor to migrate to rich countries.

As elaborated above, the human security concept and development have strong connections with trafficking in persons. Besides this, peacebuilding can also be linked to trafficking in persons. Peacebuilding assistance contains mental care, recovery, and repatriation of returned refugees, internal displaced people, and soldiers, including children. Trafficked persons are contained among those and support to such people – especially child soldiers – needs special attention because they are victims not only of the conflict but also of trafficking and exploitation (United States Department of State 2007, 24). Thus, trafficking in persons could be contextualized from human security and development, with a linkage to peacebuilding. As a transnational crime, both interstate collaboration and continuous bilateral, regional, and global networking are urgently required.

Japan's regional collaboration through bilateral cooperation projects[2]

Through JICA, Japan has contributed to the regional collaboration on human trafficking in Southeast Asia by facilitating three bilateral technical cooperation projects in Thailand, Myanmar, and Vietnam. In Thailand, JICA has conducted a two-phased bilateral technical cooperation project, with the first phase running from 2009 to 2014 and the second phase from 2015 to 2019. In addition, JICA implemented projects in Vietnam and Myanmar from 2012 to 2016. Southeast Asia is considered a hub for trafficking in persons (Shelley 2010, 141, 158; Padunchewit 2010, 3), with the situation in Thailand, especially, being complicated, as it is a victim sending, receiving, and transitioning country. The Thai government identified 824 domestic and foreign victims internally, mainly from Southeast Asia. Thailand also received back 110 Thai victims from abroad, including some from Japan and South Korea, in 2016 (Thai Government 2016).

To improve this distressing situation, the following activities were conducted under three bilateral projects. First, government officials from Thailand, Myanmar, and Vietnam joined annual regional training programs organized by JICA in Japan. Participants studied not only Japan's localized victim-centered approach and challenges but were also able to share their own approaches and difficulties. Participation of the stakeholders from both victim-sending and receiving countries helped to build trust between them. Second, JICA and its Thai counterpart agency, the Ministry of Social Development and Human Security (MSDHS), jointly held a Mekong regional workshop and invited government representatives from Cambodia, Myanmar, Laos PDR, Vietnam, as well as UN agencies and NGOs, and representatives from shelters and NGOs in Thailand. Implementation of three bilateral projects at the governmental level in the same period made it easier for the other two countries – Myanmar and Vietnam – to join the workshop and this encouraged the participation of additional countries. The workshop was held annually for eight years and, at the eighth workshop, China participated for the first time as an observer.

The trainings and workshops under the bilateral cooperation projects contributed to strengthening a regional collaboration network derived from the practitioner level. It reinforced ministerial-level frameworks such as the Coordinated Mekong Ministerial Initiative against Trafficking (COMMIT), the Japan-Thailand Joint Task Force (Japan-Thailand Joint Task Force on Counter Trafficking in Persons 2015) and Memorandum of Understanding for combatting trafficking in persons, which was concluded between the governments of Thailand and Cambodia (2003), Laos PDR (2006), Myanmar (2009), and Vietnam (2015) (Thai Government 2016, 250; Okubo and Shelley 2011).

Respecting and underpinning a local approach in three countries

The methods used to underpin the assistance were another important feature of Japan's development assistance for combatting trafficking in persons. JICA was not the main actor but played the role of facilitator to respect and enhance the different victim-centered approaches developed locally in each of the three countries. First, the project in Thailand focused on enhancing the capacity of the Multi-Disciplinary Team (MDT) members to develop more effective approaches. MDT approaches refer to a collaborative method taken by the group of professionals from diverse disciplines, including those in governments and NGOs, who come together to provide comprehensive assessments and consultations in trafficking cases (JICA Thailand 2013, 53). Members of MDT include social workers, experts from labor, health, justice, education, police, immigration, the law, foreign affairs, and so on (JICA 2012). The group is formed to achieve the same objectives through particularly planning, implementation, monitoring, and evaluation, for combatting trafficked persons in Thailand at the central and provincial levels (JICA Thailand 2013, 53).

The concept of the MDT approach appeared decades ago in Thailand. It initially took the form of bottom-up support, then a top-down protection aspect was added and, in this way, it manifested the two approaches of human security in practice. The concept first appeared in the activities of the Center for the Protection of Children's Rights (CPCR) in Bangkok for the protection and rehabilitation of victims of child abuse and neglect. The necessity of a coordinated response to the issue of victimized children prompted CPCR to develop MDT, which included provisions for legal, psychological, and social welfare services (Padunchewit 2010, 10). Then, the Asia Foundation (TAF) also adopted an MDT approach, incorporating a gender-sensitive and human-rights-based approach, along with empowerment to increase the victims' choices. MDT, as developed by TAF, is comprised of medical practitioners, social workers, translators, NGOs, media people, prosecutors, police, shelters, lawyers, and others (Padunchewit 2010, 18, 31). Then, MSDHS added government officials to the MDT membership and, as a result, the MDT approach has become a comprehensive mechanism for rescue, protection, and rehabilitation of the victims, embodying both top-down protection and bottom-up empowerment. This mechanism could therefore be considered a human security approach.

In JICA's technical cooperation project in Thailand, the Japanese experts tried to enhance as far as possible the potential of the MDT approach derived from local contexts. The provision of Japanese experts, along with trainings and workshops in Thailand and Japan, were effective in developing the coordination mechanisms of MDT and, for participants, in increasing skills for implementing the victim-centered approach. Five Japanese experts stayed with the MSDHS for one or two years (long-term experts), covering the whole five years of phase one, while 15 experts were dispatched for periods of ten days to a month (short-term experts). The long-term experts were posted as chief advisors and project coordinators and covered the field of anti-human-trafficking and social reintegration. They played the role of facilitators among member organizations of MDT. The short-term experts joined the workshops and trainings held by the project and introduced the

Japanese government's policies and measures against human trafficking, methods for nurturing case managers, and so on. More than 50 MDT members participated in the training sessions in Japan.

Through trainings and workshops, MDT members came to trust each other, developed an understanding of the roles of other organizations, and learned better methods of communicating with the victims. Improvement of the quality of services for the victims is difficult to measure, and the positive effects may not be directly observable, apart from setting up the legal framework or increasing the numbers of prosecutions. However, the victims felt more satisfaction with MDT's service at the end of the first phase compared to the beginning of this project (JICA Thailand 2013). Through the cooperation project, some former Thai victims joined workshops and trainings and shared their experiences with the stakeholders regarding protection. This helped the stakeholders to develop an understanding of how to communicate with the victims based on their own needs. Furthermore, some former victims empowered themselves to form an NGO to support other victims.

Second, in Myanmar, JICA conducted a technical cooperation project to enhance the capacity of social workers from victim support agencies. Unlike other donors, Japan did not push the Myanmar government toward quick democratization and, as a result, a trust-based relationship was fostered between both governments. This enabled the Myanmar government to make an official request to conduct this project. During the project, 72 trainers were nurtured, and they started to conduct their own trainings, lectures, and educational events in their workplaces and communities. They also shared their newly acquired attitudes, skills, and knowledge with a wide range of people. All of the trainings for the social workers incorporated the communication skills and attitudinal changes of trainees toward victims. Before the training, many social workers had little knowledge about how to deal with the returnees and thought of them as "trouble-makers." However, through training, they came to understand the issue of trafficking in persons, learned better social work skills, and changed their attitude toward the returnees. Better communications between social workers and the returnees have led to joint activities to grow vegetables, make handicrafts, as well as visiting the market and pagodas together and those have fostered the trust between them and promoted the recovery of the returnees (JICA, forthcoming).

Third, in Vietnam, there was a growing demand for the provision of appropriate information about safe migration and measures to prevent trafficking, as well as counseling services and social reintegration of the victims. Some NGOs operated a telephone service designed to stop trafficking in persons, but it only lasted for a limited period. Others operated a hotline as a part of the provincial government's services. This operation, however, lacked proper coordination among the relevant organizations such as the police, shelters, and so on. The Ministry of Labor, Invalids and Social Affairs also operated a child helpline in Hanoi from 2004. There were calls to strengthen the functions of the established child helpline and to expand its functions to serve as an anti-trafficking in persons hotline designed for the prevention of trafficking as well as to provide support for the social reintegration of trafficked persons.

The project aimed to support the establishment of a hotline service, strengthen referral mechanisms between concerned organizations, increase capacity development among counseling staff, and raise public awareness of the hotline (JICA 2017). In this project, the Japanese experts contributed as facilitators to the efforts undertaken by the Vietnamese government. Three long-term and five short-term experts were assigned as chief advisors, project coordinators, and – in the fields of social work – case management, system design, information education, and communication. Training was also provided for telephone counseling, hotline management, and hotline operations, along with the equipment necessary for the establishing the hotline. More than 20 project stakeholders joined the workshops and trainings in Thailand and Japan (JICA 2017). The Vietnamese Anti-TIP Hotline started its operations in October 2013 and, in 2017, local news reported that there were nearly 10,000 calls to the hotline. Of these, 232 calls were referred immediately to the police for investigation, resulting in the rescue of 92 victims (Customs News 2017). Moreover, in An Giang province, almost 5,000 calls related to human trafficking were received by the hotline (Vietnam News 2016).

Throughout these three projects, Japan not only shared its know-how with the recipient governments but underpinned their approach as a backseat player. Japan was even able to learn from MDT approach. The Japanese long-term experts acted not as teachers or donors but as facilitators or catalysts. This back-support type of cooperation was derived from a victim-centered approach based on a human security perspective. It enabled a strengthening of both the donor and recipient side's weak points and thus could be a unique approach within development cooperation.

Lessons learned

In conclusion, there are two major findings that fit with the theme of this chapter. First, based on multi-layered trust, regional networking through bilateral cooperation with each of the three countries was fostered among the victims, MDT members in Thailand, staff for hotlines in Vietnam, social workers in Myanmar, and Japanese experts. Without such trust, some victims would have been unable to share their experiences at the workshop in Thailand. The networking strengthened relationships between countries that both send and receive the victims of trafficking and will help these countries to work together to address future threats.

Second, respect for local approaches requires a donor to be a supporter, not the main actor. The MDT approach was developed in Thailand from a bottom-up basis and expanded to involve top-down aspects. A hotline was developed for use in the Vietnamese context. The main foci of each of the technical cooperation projects were set up based on the victims' needs and the structure of these victim-centered approaches – thus demonstrating human security in practice. In Myanmar, as a trusted country (Kapucu 2011, 12), Japan was able to conduct assistance. Japan's attitude of supporting the local context not as the main actor but as facilitator led to the success of three projects and contributed to improving the quality of existing mechanisms for combatting trafficking in persons.

Human security in practice 2: peacebuilding assistance in Mindanao

Japan has been involved in the Mindanao peace process between the Philippine government and MILF (Moro Islamic Liberation Front) since 2006. Like other peacebuilding operations, the initial hurdle to overcome was the one of sovereignty. This was followed by other concerns, such as modalities and target groups that were necessary in order to promote human security. This section will scrutinize how Japan overcame the sovereignty issue of the Philippines and what kinds of new implementation measures Japan/JICA was able to create on the ground to maximize the effect of human security.

Mindanao conflict and Japan's commitment to its peace process

Although it would be better to illustrate the conflict in Mindanao and its peace process in detail, the limited space here will only permit a summary of the key points. The roots of the conflict in Mindanao can be traced back to the legacy of the Spanish and American colonization of the Philippines between the 16th and 20th centuries. During the occupation by the US, new land laws and the public administration benefitted mainstream Christian Filipinos and played a role in the destruction of the traditional political institutions of Moros (Santos 2010, 60–1). After full independence was achieved in 1946, the policy introduced by President Marcos of promoting migration to Mindanao aggravated territorial disputes between Christian migrants and Muslim inhabitants. By the mid-1960s the number of Christian migrants exceeded the Muslim population, which lacked proper recognition of its identity, cultural values, physical security, sufficient livelihood, and equal participation in the modern Philippines (Lingga 2005; Ferrer 2005; Jubair 2007).

In 1968, the Jabidah Massacre in Corregidor triggered armed Moro resistance (Ferrer 2005, 10; Lam 2009, 76). Over the next 40 years, the struggle continued, with fluctuations in intensity and frequency of violence, as well as changes in issues and actors. The Moro National Liberation Front (MNLF) was established in 1969 and a factional group, the MILF, subsequently separated from the MNLF around 1976 due to disagreements over the position of the MNLF toward the Tripoli Agreement of 1976. The MILF's struggle continued until the Comprehensive Agreement for Bangsamoro (CAB) was concluded with the Philippine government in March 2014.

Different Philippine administrations took different measures to deal with the conflict until the CAB was finally realized. In the restricted context of Japan's commitment to the Mindanao peace process with the MILF, the Gloria Macapagal-Arroyo administration (2000–2010) and the administration of Benigno Aquino Jr. (2010–2016) were two significantly important partners involved in pursuing peace in Mindanao, for eight years altogether. Japan's involvement started with its participation in the Malaysian-led International Monitoring Team (IMT) for socioeconomic assistance in 2006. Japan's participation in the IMT expanded the nature of the country's assistance by navigating Japan's assistance to a new type of 3D (defense, diplomacy, and development) (Uesugi 2015, 12). A series of domestic processes was assigned to Japanese IMT members, which made this type of 3D assistance possible. Basically, JICA staff members were assigned to take on a role in the socioeconomic component of the IMT. They were, however, initially seconded to the Ministry of Foreign Affairs and were then made Secretaries of the Japanese Embassy in Manila prior to being attached to the IMT headquarters in Cotabato, Mindanao. In this way, Japanese members of the IMT had three different titles – namely JICA staff members for ODA, diplomats for diplomacy, and IMT members for socioeconomic tasks. They made the most use of the three titles to connect defense, diplomacy, and development in the context of Japan's assistance.

Japan's participation in the IMT was also very much related to the discussion of the issue of Philippine sovereignty as well as collaboration between R2P and human security. Another aspect that deserves highlighting was the use of mediation fora, which aimed to connect top-down and bottom-up approaches as new implementation measures for human security.

Philippine sovereignty and Japan

One of the dilemmas of human security in ODA practices was finding ways to deal with the sovereignty of a recipient country. When human security became a core principle for Japan's peacebuilding assistance in 2003 onwards, JICA faced a challenge in developing the means to swiftly reach out to direct beneficiaries. While it was imperative for human security to respect the sovereignty of a target country, people-centered operations that extended beyond traditional government-to-government assistance were also required to practice the human security concept. In the case of the Mindanao peace process, the Philippine government – especially the Arroyo administration onwards with the consent of the MILF – showed a strong political will to pursue long-lasting peace with necessary assistance from third parties, so that the contradictions between sovereignty and human security were minimal. The development of a trust relationship between the Philippine stakeholders and Japan also helped to overcome the possible resurgence of the sovereignty problem when the peace process reached a stalemate in 2008.

After the failure of negotiations between the administration of Fidel Ramos (1992–1998) and the subsequent all-out war launched by the short-lived Estrada administration (1998–2000), the peace process was finally internationalized during the Arroyo administration, wherein the government and the MILF agreed to pursue peace without compromising Philippine sovereignty. Initially, Malaysia was invited to be the facilitator of their negotiations. The Malaysia-led IMT was deployed to guarantee the cease-fire agreement between the antagonists. International society respected the sovereignty of the Philippines and supported consensus-building between the antagonists with ample flexibility in decision-making. When Japan was invited to take part in the IMT in 2006, there was a consensus in decision-making between the government, the MILF, and Malaysia, and thus there was no observable infringement of Philippine sovereignty (Lam 2009, 82).

As opposed to its participation in the IMT, implementation of socioeconomic assistance was a more acute sovereignty-related issue for Japan due to the fact that ODA actors, in principle, were not allowed to engage with a rebel group to provide socioeconomic assistance. This problem was solved without any effects on Philippine sovereignty when the Arroyo administration, with the consent of the MILF, encouraged international communities to engage with the Bangsamoro Development Agency (BDA) to provide rehabilitation and development works in Mindanao (Arroyo 2006). The BDA was the development arm of the MILF. It was a pleasant surprise to the international donor community that the government supported rehabilitation and development in the territory of a rebel group before a final peace agreement was in place.

The trust relationship between the Philippines and Japan also overcame the issue of sovereignty when the peace process reached a stalemate in 2008. The peace process was, in fact, on the verge of being abandoned due to the long-standing issue of the ancestral domains. In an insecure situation, with numerous armed clashes, Japan decided to stay on to continue its assistance in the conflict-affected areas while assistance from other external agencies was suspended, and they withdrew from Mindanao. Although Japan made the decision for a good cause, a favorable response was also necessary from the Philippines so that issues did not emerge between the two countries related to infringement of Philippine sovereignty. This provided the basis for the development of trust between the two nations that enabled Japan to sustain her assistance in Mindanao without provoking any negative repercussions from the Philippine side.

Collaboration between R2P and human security

The hybrid nature of the IMT in Mindanao has implied a possible common ground between the concept of human security and pillar two of R2P, which is the dimension of international cooperation for preventing atrocities and genocides (United Nations 2014). Japan's assistance for the Mindanao peace process, including participation in the IMT, was justified by its idealistic aspiration to engage in conflict-affected areas with the concept of human security – aside from its own political self-contentment. On the other hand, Malaysia undertook a new type of observation mission for the first time in Mindanao. A former head of IMT articulated that the IMT was regarded as part of a pillar two mechanism.[3]

The UN initiated a series of discussions about the three pillars of R2P, which was concluded in July 2014. These were submitted to the General Assembly in the report of UN Secretary-General titled "Fulfilling Our Collective Responsibility: International Assistance and the R2P" (A/68/947-S/2014/449) (United Nations 2014). This report focused on pillar two and articulated the core concept and forms of assistance. One section reads "while traditional development cooperation has a role to play, assistance to States in the context of the R2P will also involve a wider range of economic, political, humanitarian and, in certain cases, military tools" (United Nations 2014). In the Southeast Asian region, the Association of Southeast Asian Nations (ASEAN) responded to paragraphs 138–140 of the 2005 World Summit Outcome Document on R2P and eventually established the High-Level Advisory Panel on R2P in 2013 to contribute ideas for the strengthening of regional capacity for R2P (High Level Advisory Panel on the Responsibility to Protect in Southeast Asia 2014).

Long before these movements of the UN and ASEAN, it was observed that both Malaysia and Japan had their own intentions and justification to work together in the same monitoring team. It was, however, subsequently described as a hybrid measure to collaborate between the concepts of R2P and human security. For Malaysia, Japan's participation in the IMT followed the objective of pillar two in principle but took different implementation procedures by avoiding involvement in any UN mechanisms. Japan's socio-economic assistance was regarded to be a security measure for non-armed IMT members while monitoring cease-fire conditions in conflict-affected areas. Due to visible needs-survey activities and assistance by Japanese IMT members, positive credit was also shared by the whole IMT, and this increased the acceptance rate of the IMT by local communities. For Japan, on the other hand, the security measure provided by the monitoring component of the IMT was indispensable in order to step into insecure areas to conduct needs surveys. Based on this arrangement, Japan was able to reach out to vulnerable communities for people-centered assistance.

The mutual support between both of the components of the IMT – monitoring cease-fire conditions and the socioeconomic program – showed the potential contribution of human security to pillar two of R2P outside the UN arena. Nonetheless, all these arrangements were endorsed by the Philippine side. The Philippine government always had the final say. This new mindset could therefore suggest an alternative way for Japan to contribute to peacekeeping aside from deploying the Self Defense Forces for United Nations Peacekeeping Operations (UNPKO).

Mediation fora to connect top-down and bottom-up approaches

The vulnerable cease-fire conditions involved JICA in another empowerment measure for local communities, aside from its usual mandate of development assistance. As already discussed in the previous section, when the peace process reached a stalemate in 2008, Japan remained in Mindanao and continued to provide assistance. If the security situation had deteriorated and the peace process had stalled for a considerable time, there was a risk that assistance programs would be terminated. While continuing its projects in insecure conditions, JICA sought to find alternative ways to revive the peace process in alignment with rehabilitation and development works. Within JICA, views emerged that the agency needed to change its mindset and should be involved in peacemaking to some extent in order to break the deadlock. It was therefore decided to provide local actors with an opportunity to empower themselves to act in support of the resurgence of the peace process. JICA, in collaboration with Malaysia Science University therefore organized track-two and track-one-and-a-half mediation fora called Consolidation of Peace for Mindanao (COP) in 2009, 2012, and 2014.

The main objective of COP was to address how civil society groups in Mindanao could contribute to the peace process. The first and second COP fora – focused exclusively on Mindanao – were organized in Penang, Malaysia, where participants could have informal and frank discussions in a relaxing atmosphere. Some 50 participants attended from Manila, various parts of Mindanao, and elsewhere. For COP in 2009, the discussion theme was how civil society groups could help to put the peace process back on track.[4] With this objective, nine concurrent workshop sessions and a couple of plenary sessions were convened for participants to discuss various issues among themselves. Although that forum took track-two (the epistemic communities including academics, religious leaders, and journalists) and track-three (civil society such as grassroots organizations and issue-oriented advocacy groups) approaches, official track-one players, including the chief negotiator of the MILF, attended as observers. It is important to note that the approach used in the COP aimed to mobilize track-two actors (middle-range leadership) to connect track-one (top leadership) and track-three (grassroots leadership) actors, as Lederach (1997) suggested.

After COP in 2009, the participants started the consultative process with both the Philippine government and the MILF (Askandar and Abubakar 2009, 150–1). The consultative process, in fact, connected the bottom-up approach by empowering local stakeholders with the top-down approach of the peace negotiators. A channel of communication between the local communities and the peace process was finally established. COP in 2012 followed the same approach as that of 2009 while COP in 2014 was promoted to be a track-one-and-a-half forum in Hiroshima with the participation of the chairman of the MILF and the presidential advisor for the peace process. The presence of President Aquino in the middle of COP 2014 endorsed its importance and value. Participants concentrated on discussing the implementation measures of the newly concluded Comprehensive Agreement for Bangsamoro (CAB).

A series of COP fora supported Wennmann's observation that "there was a growing recognition in the development community for the potential role of mediation outside its traditional role in conflict resolution" (Wennmann 2011, 94). JICA shifted from the role of a development agency away from merely providing economic assistance, to being a more reliable partner in coping with the political dimensions of peacebuilding. The trust Japan gained from local stakeholders during the exercise of socioeconomic empowerment helped JICA to overcome its limited mandate and allowed the agency to undertake new measures in connecting top-down and bottom-up approaches.

Lessons learned

Some lessons can be extracted from Japan's assistance in Mindanao in view of human security as follows. First, the respect for Philippine sovereignty and the trust relationship between Japan and the Philippines lowered the hurdles to addressing human security in Japan's assistance for the Mindanao peace process.

Second, although based on policies and implementation guidelines on human security in Japan's ODA, new measures were created and implemented to further address human security in accordance with local conditions. The unintended synergetic effects between R2P and human security in the activities of the IMT provides some empirical evidence of this, along with the creation of mediation fora by the development agency.

Conclusion

This chapter has examined Japan's contribution to the intertwined ideas of peacebuilding, development, and human security. The main finding for this chapter is that human security, in the view of the Japanese government, has played different roles at different levels. First, at the multilateral engagement level, human security has become an international norm and the concept has been distinct from R2P. For Japan, joining the discussion on the concept of human security from the beginning allowed the country to regain its position in the international community. This was part of Japan's efforts to avoid the risk of becoming isolated from the donor community, although, in practice, Japan continued to take sensitive approaches to recipient countries so as not to jeopardize good relationships. Second, at the development assistance level, human security has played a role as a guiding principle for Japan's ODA. ODA was used as a tool for Japan's international contributions in contrast to military enforcement by allied Western countries. The concept of human security and its implementation guidelines have been refined by policy-practice interactions between MOFA and JICA. The process of interaction between policy and practice was also employed when implementing development assistance projects. While still drawing from the Human Development Index and other statistics to establish an overall picture of the country, at a practical level, the approach involved adapting development assistance programs to suit local contexts.

Third, at a practical level, the concept of human security has been interpreted and applied in accordance with diversified local contexts. In consequence, the people-centered approach and a set of flexible measures to respond to local needs have sometimes created new ways of implementation. While still in line with ODA policies, they seem to have extended beyond initial expectations. In both case studies, the trust-based relationship between Japan and the partner countries allowed Japan to optimize its way of handling issues in accordance with local contexts. In addressing the trafficking of persons in Southeast Asia, Japanese experts maintained their support roles as facilitators while letting local partners take initiatives in responding to this issue so that the capacity of the partner organizations could be enhanced. Conducting three bilateral cooperation projects together helped in fostering a regional network among concerned agencies that consisted of victim-receiving and sending countries. For Mindanao, in the Philippines, collaboration between Japan's human-security-based assistance and IMT's initial mandate, according to pillar two of R2P, was seen as a hybrid of the peacekeeping mission. The mediation activity was another new modality for JICA as a development agency.

The two core concepts that underpin Japan's ODA – respecting sovereignty in collaboration with multiple stakeholders and abrogating the use of military force – have been well received by the international community. The Japanese approach to partner countries, introduced through the two case studies in this chapter, shows the improvement of the situation of people left behind based on the local context and will indirectly contribute to reducing human fragility and improving human security. There are, however, further challenges ahead for Japan, including how to promote the concept of human security and its practice domestically, and how to further develop good practices in providing assistance which respects both state sovereignty and human security. The core approach of Japan's ODA has now been tested.

Notes

1 This chapter does not necessarily represent the opinions of the authors' affiliation.
2 Author would like to express her appreciation to Harue Tomino, staff of Bureau of Gender Equality and Poverty Reduction in JICA, for her cooperation in this section.
3 Author interviewed a former head of the IMT, Maj. Gen. Datuk Mahdi Yusof in Kuala Lumpur, Malaysia on August 26, 2015.
4 Author interviewed Professor Kamarulzaman Askandar in Kota Kinabalu, Malaysia on August 28, 2015.

References

Arroyo, G. M. (2006) "A meeting of the Philippine Consultative Group and other stakeholders" *Speech Presented at the 2006 Philippine Development Forum* March 30, Tagaytay City.

Askandar, K. and Abubakar, A. (2009) *Peace for Mindanao* Unit of Research and Education for Peace, Universiti Sains Malaysia and Southeast Asian Conflict Studies Network, Penang.

Beeks, K. and Amir, D. eds. (2006) *Trafficking and the Global Sex Industry* Lexington Books, Oxford.

Boutros-Ghali, B. (1992) *An Agenda for Peace: Preventive Diplomacy, Peacemaking and Peacekeeping* Report of the UN Secretary-General, A/47/277–S/24111.

Camilleri, J. A. (2000) "The security dilemma revisited: Implications for the Asia-Pacific" in Tow, W. T., Thakur, R. and Hyun, I. eds., *Asia's Emerging Regional*

Order: Reconciling Traditional and Human Security The United Nations University, New York 306–10.

Commission on Human Security (2003) *Human Security Now: Protecting and Empowering People* United Nations, New York.

Customs News (2017) *JICA Continues Supports to Fight Human Trafficking in Vietnam* (http://customsnews.vn/jica-continues-supports-to-fight-human-trafficking-in-Vietnam-4211.html) Accessed July 20, 2018.

Dan, Y. (2000) "A brief review of human security" *Human Security* 4(1999/2000) 325–9.

Edström, B. (2009) *Japan and the Challenge of Human Security: The Foundation of a New Policy 1995–2003* Institute for Security and Development Policy, Stockholm.

——— (2011) *Japan and Human Security: The Derailing of a Foreign Policy Vision* Institute for Security and Development Policy, Stockholm.

Ferrer, M. C. (2005) "The Philippine State and Moro Resistance" in Kamarulzaman, A. and Ayesah, A. eds., *The Mindanao Conflict* Southeast Asian Conflict Studies Network, Penang 1–30.

Fukushima, A. (2004) "Human security and Japanese foreign policy" *UNESCO, International Conference on Human Security in East Asia: 16–17 June 2003, Seoul, Republic of Korea: Proceedings* UNESCO, Korean National Commission for UNESCO and Ilmin International Relations Institute of Korea University, Seoul 121–67.

Funabashi, Y. (1990) "Japan and the new world order" *Foreign Affairs* 70(5) Winter 55–74.

High Level Advisory Panel on the Responsibility to Protect in Southeast Asia (2014) *Mainstreaming the Responsibility to Protect in Southeast Asia: Pathway towards a Caring ASEAN Community* United Nations, New York.

Japan International Cooperation Agency (JICA) (2012) *Tackling Human Trafficking in the Mekong Subregion* (www.jica.go.jp/english/news/field/2011/20120302_01.html) Accessed July 28, 2018.

——— (2017) *Betonamu Shakaishugikyouwakoku Jinshintorihikitaisaku Hottorainnikakaru Taiseiseibi Projekuto Shurojihyoukachousa Houkokusho* [Joint Terminal Evaluation Report for Project for the Establishment of Anti-Trafficking in Persons Hotline in Vietnam] JICA, Tokyo.

——— (forthcoming) *Myanmar koku Jinshintorihiki Higaisha Jiritsushiennotameno Noryokukojo Projekuto Shuryojihyoukachousa Houkokusho* [Joint Terminal Evaluation Report for Project on Capacity Improvement of Recovery and Reintegration Assistance for Trafficked Persons] JICA, Tokyo.

Japan-Thailand Joint Task Force on Counter Trafficking in Persons (2015) *Japan-Thailand Joint Press Statement on the Occasion of the Visit by Prime Minister Prayut Chan-o-Cha of the Kingdom of Thailand to Japan* February 9, Tokyo (www.mofa.go.jp/files/000067642.pdf) Accessed July 29, 2018.

JICA Thailand (2013) *Tai Okoku Jinshintorihiki Higaishahogo Jiritsushien Projekuto Shuryojihyoukachousa Houkokusho* [The Terminal Evaluation Report for the Project on Strengthening of Multi-Disciplinary Teams (MDTs) for Protection of Trafficked Persons in Thailand] JICA Thailand Office, Bangkok.

Jonsson, A. ed. (2009) *Human Trafficking and Human Security* Routledge, Oxon.

Jubair, S. (2007) *The Long Road to Peace: Inside the GRP-MILF Peace Process* Institute of Bangsamoro Studies, Davao.

Kamidohzono, S. G., Gómez, O. A., and Mine, Y. (2016) "Embracing human security: New directions of Japan's ODA for the 21st century" in Kato, H., Page, J. and Shimomura, Y. eds., *Japan's Development Assistance: Foreign Aid and the Post-2015 Agenda* Palgrave Macmillan, Basingstoke 205–21.

Kapucu, N. (2011) "Collaborative governance in international disasters: Nargis Cyclone in Myanmar and Sichuan earthquake in China cases" *International Journal of Emergency Management* 8 (1) 1–25.

Kitaoka, S. (2007) *Kokuren no seiji rikigaku: Nihon wa doko ni iru no ka [The Political Dynamics of the UN: Where Does Japan Stand?]* Chuo Koron Shinsha, Tokyo.

Kurusu, K. (2016) "Does the concept of human security generate additional value? An analysis of Japanese stakeholder perceptions" *JICA-RI Working Paper No. 122* JICA Research Institute, Tokyo (www.jica.go.jp/jica-ri/publication/working-paper/jrft3q00000027jd-att/JICA-RI_WP_No.122.pdf) Accessed July 19, 2018.

Lam, P. E. (2009) *Japan's Peace-Building Diplomacy in Asia* Routledge, Oxon.

Lederach, J. P. (1997) *Building Peace* United States Institute of Peace, Washington, DC.

Lincoln, E. J. (1993) *Japan's New Global Role* Brookings Institution, Washington, DC.

Lingga, A. S. M. (2005) "Mindanao peace process: The need for a new formula" in Askandar, K. and Abubakar, A. eds., *The Mindanao Conflict* Southeast Asian Conflict Studies Network, Penang 33–50.

Ministry of Foreign Affairs of Japan (MOFA) (1992) "Japan's official development assistance charter before revision (approved by the cabinet in June 1992)" *MOFA, Japan's Official Development Assistance White Paper 2004* Ministry of Foreign Affairs, Tokyo.

——— (1999) "Japan's medium-term policy on official development" (www.mofa.go.jp/policy/oda/mid-term/1999/index.html) Accessed July 15, 2018.

——— (2003) *Japan's Official Development Assistance Charter* (www.mofa.go.jp/policy/oda/reform/revision0308.pdf) Accessed July 17, 2018.

——— (2004) *Japan's Official Development Assistance White Paper 2004* Ministry of Foreign Affairs, Tokyo.

——— (2006) *Chair's Summary "Friends of Human Security" Meeting* October 19 Millennium United Nations Plaza Hotel, New York (www.mofa.go.jp/policy/human_secu/friends/summary0610.html) Accessed July 11, 2018.

——— (2007) *"What the Friends of Human Security Aims to Achieve: Measure Progress by Change in the Lives of People"* By H. E. Mr. Yukio Takasu, Ambassador of Japan in Charge of Human Security on the Occasion of 9th Ministerial Meeting of the Human Security Network May 18, Ljubljana (www.mofa.go.jp/policy/human_secu/state0705.html) Accessed July 10, 2018.

——— (2015) *Cabinet Decision on the Development Cooperation Charter* (www.mofa.go.jp/files/000067701.pdf) Accessed July 15, 2018.

94   *Ako Muto and Sachiko Ishikawa*

——— (2016) *Friends of Human Security* (www.mofa.go.jp/policy/human_secu/friends/index.html) Accessed July 15, 2018.

——— (2017) *White Paper on Development Cooperation 2016* Ministry of Foreign Affairs, Tokyo.

Newman, E. (2013) "The challenge of human security policymaking" in Tow, W. T., Walton, D. and Kersten, R. eds., *New Approaches to Human Security in the Asia-Pacific: China, Japan and Austria* Ashgate, Farnham Surrey 213–23.

Okubo, S. and Shelley, L. eds. (2011) *Human Security, Transnational Crime and Human Trafficking: Asian and Western Perspectives* Routledge, Oxon.

Padunchewit, J. (2010) "Crafting strategic communication to combat trafficking of women and children in Thailand: The case of the Asia Foundation" *NIDA Case Research Journal* 2(1) 1–43.

Santos, S. M. (2010) "War and peace on the Moro Front: Three standard bearers, three forms of struggle, three tracks (overview)" in Rodriguez, D. ed., *Primed and Purposeful: Armed Groups and Human Security Efforts in the Philippines* Graduate Institute of International and Development Studies, Geneva 58–90.

Shelley, L. (2010) *Human Trafficking: A Global Perspective* Cambridge University Press, New York.

Tadokoro, M. (1997) "Between the West and Asia: Japan's position on human rights issues" in Schmiegelow, M. ed., *Democracy in Asia* Campus Verlag and St. Martin's Press, Frankfurt and New York 255–73.

Tanaka, A. (2002) "Anzen hosho no saiteki kosuto; taichu wa taisho zengen wo" [Minimum cost for security: Aid to China should be gradually reduced], *Asahi Shimbun* September 27.

Thai Government (2016) *Thailand's Country Report on Anti-Human Trafficking Response* January 1–December 31 (www.jica.go.jp/project/thailand/016/materials/ku57pq00001yw2db-att/thailands_country_report_01.pdf) Accessed August 7, 2018.

Uesugi, Y. (2015) "Wahei shien deno gaikou to kaihatsu no renkei: Mindanao wahei ni okeru heiwa no haitou no katsuyou to kokusai kanshidan no yakuwari no kousatsu" [Coordination between diplomacy and development in the Mindanao peace process: A Study of the Use of 'Peace Dividends' and Roles of International Monitoring Team] in Uesugi, Y. ed., *Nihon no kokusai heiwa kyouryoku seisaku to jissen no kiseki [A Short History of Japan's Policy and Practice on International Peace Cooperation]* Waseda University, Tokyo 1–19.

United Nations (UN) (2000) "Protocol to prevent, suppress and punish trafficking in persons especially women and children" *Annex I of General Assembly Resolution on 55/25* United Nations Convention against Transnational Organized Crime (A/RES/55/25) November 10 United Nations, New York.

——— (2005) *In Larger Freedom: Towards Development, Security and Human Rights for All* Report of the Secretary-General (A/59/2005/Add.3) May 26, United Nations, New York.

——— (2012) *General Assembly Resolution on Follow-Up to Paragraph 143 on Human Security of the 2005 World Summit Outcome* (A/RES/66/290) October 25 United Nations, New York.

———— (2014) *Report of the Secretary-General on Fulfilling Our Collective Responsibility: International Assistance and the Responsibility to Protect* (A/68/947-S/2014/449) United Nations, New York.

United States Department of State (2002) *Trafficking in Persons Report* (www.state.gov/j/tip/rls/tiprpt/2002/index.htm) Accessed July 29, 2018.

———— (2007) *Trafficking in Persons Report* (www.state.gov/j/tip/rls/tiprpt/2007/index.htm) Accessed July 29, 2018.

———— (2016) *Trafficking in Persons Report* (www.state.gov/j/tip/rls/tiprpt/2016/index.htm) Accessed July 29, 2018.

Vietnam News (2016) *Human Trafficking Hotline a Success* (http://Vietnamnews.vn/society/282795/human-trafficking-hotline-a-success.html#6jsAYoK16zYo TRtR.97) Accessed August 7, 2018.

Wennmann, A. (2011) *The Political Economy of Peacemaking* Routledge, Oxon.

World Bank (1993) *The East Asian Miracle: Economic Growth and Public Policy* Oxford University Press, New York.

Yasumoto, D. T. (1995) *The New Multilateralism in Japan's Foreign Policy* Macmillan, London.

5 South Korea's middle power diplomacy in development and human security[1]

Eun Mee Kim, Brendan Howe,
Seon Young Bae, and Ji Hyun Shin

South Korea as a middle power

South Korea's "power" status in foreign affairs is broadly recognized as being that of a middle power, both in terms of internal perceptions, as well as how it is perceived by the world and in particular by its regional neighbors. South Korea is the only country that has successfully transformed from a nation with extreme poverty to prosperity since the UN was founded in 1945. It has achieved that to which many developing countries still aspire for their nation: economic development, democracy, and peace. Although peace and security on the Korean peninsula is yet to be fully achieved, South Korea's prosperity and relative peace within the framework of an armistice are the source of admiration for many developing countries that are faced with double challenges of poverty and war/conflict. This chapter presents the extent to which South Korea has directly engaged in its middle power niche diplomacy with development and human security, two of the three key elements of with which this volume deals, and, through spillover, indirectly with the third, peacebuilding (see Chapters 1 and 2).

South Korea's development cooperation, in particular its official development assistance (ODA), has become an important tool for its diplomacy since it joined the OECD's Development Assistance Committee in 2010. Its volume of ODA has been growing steadily, while that of many other countries has been decreasing in light of the ongoing global economic crisis, and populist or conservative governments that have turned more inward toward their domestic constituency. Therefore, South Korea's growing diplomatic power may be attributed to this rising ODA volume. But more importantly, South Korea is the proud poster-child of post–World War II economic development, democracy, and peace, which has made it a sought-after development partner for many developing countries. Furthermore, the South Korean government has not been shy about declaring that its ODA is based on South Korea's own development experience and has developed ODA projects with an explicit goal of expediting such knowledge-based technology transfers (Stallings and Kim 2017).

South Korea's history as a large ODA recipient in its post–Korean War development also provides insight into its interest in human security. Successive South Korean governments have used the rhetoric that it is the only country that has successfully become a donor from being a large recipient of ODA, and the government constantly reminds the South Korean public that they have a responsibility to pay back a debt to the world that has supported them during hard times of poverty and war. Thus, it has provided considerable ODA with a focus on human security even though it does not explicitly use the term (Kim, Bae, and Shin 2018).

This chapter is organized as follows: first, we examine South Korea's foreign policy through ODA since 2010 when it became an OECD DAC member; second, we review South Korea's promotion of human security through its ODA (and other policy vehicles); and finally, we conclude with an analysis of South Korea's engagement as a middle power in its diplomacy.

South Korea's diplomacy and ODA

South Korea's history as a recipient of ODA dates back to 1945 when it began to receive support from the US after World War II as a former colony of war powers. South Korea's ODA volume reached US$12.78 billion from 1945 to 1995 when it finally graduated from being a recipient (ODA Korea 2018). ODA was particularly significant during and after the Korean War (1950–1953) when it received huge economic and military assistance. Postwar reconstruction ODA was important for the nation to rebuild itself after the devastating war that destroyed nearly 80 percent of its economic capacity (Kim 1997). Since South Korea was a resource-poor nation with little capital or technology, it required foreign capital for its reconstruction and economic development. The foreign capital in the form of ODA was critical for the nation's economic development (*ibid.*). It is perhaps not surprising, therefore, given South Korea's own success, that economic development has played a central role in policy initiatives aimed at influencing global discourse and the international governance agenda, reflecting both national interest and an operational niche within which South Korea can punch above its weight.

With rapid economic development and poverty reduction in a generation, South Korea was able to become a donor of ODA by the late 1980s. In 1987, it established the Economic Development and Cooperation Fund at the Korea Export-Import (ExIm) Bank to handle concessional loans, and in 1991, it established the Korea International Cooperation Agency

(KOICA) to administer grant aid. The Roh Moo-hyun government (2003–2008) declared its wish to join the OECD's Development Assistance Committee (DAC), which is considered the club of advanced industrialized countries with substantial volume of ODA. In 2009, DAC members decided to accept South Korea as its 24th member, and in 2010, South Korea became a member of OECD DAC. In accordance with its new DAC responsibilities, South Korea is looking to expand dramatically its ODA budget and also to host many fact-finding missions and students from small- and medium-sized regional economies, who see in the ROK a role model more closely analogous to their own conditions and experiences than perhaps is the case with more traditional donors. Furthermore, South Korea is unique among donors in not suffering from any neo-imperial baggage. Thus, for Soyeon Kim (2011, 805), "the Korean ODA model in particular epitomises Seoul's strategic positioning (or bridging) between the developed and developing countries. With the model, Korea promotes its distinctive approach to aid while at the same time proclaiming its willingness to be part of global aid efforts."

Even before joining the OECD DAC, "Korea had emerged as the unrivalled leading donor, in absolute amounts, among non-DAC OECD countries" (Chun, Munyi, and Lee 2010, 790). By the time of the first DAC peer review of Korea in 2012, the country had trebled its ODA over the preceding five years to US$1,325 million per year or 0.12 percent of its gross national income (GNI), and it had committed to a further doubling by 2015 (OECD 2012). In 2012, Korea's ODA amounted to US$1,597.5 million (net disbursement), of which US$1,183.2 million was bilateral aid and US$414.3 million was multilateral aid. Grants amounted to US$714.9 million (60.4 percent) and loans to US$468.3 million (39.6 percent) of the total. In fact, in 2012, under conditions of financial crisis, Korea had the largest increase in ODA among the DAC at 17 percent, far ahead of Australia's 9.2 percent, the next largest increase, whereas most DAC members decreased their ODA that year (Roehrig 2013).

President Lee Myung-bak (2008–2013) continued the strong push for ODA initiated by the Roh government, although their political stances were very different. Lee headed a business-friendly conservative government in contrast to Roh's pro-labor progressive government. Despite these differences in political orientation, Lee eagerly supported Roh's plan to gain membership in the OECD DAC. When South Korea became a member, the Lee government promoted the use of ODA in pursuit of its "Global Korea" foreign policy. The legal foundation for South Korea's ODA is the Framework Act on International Development Cooperation (hereinafter, Framework Act) promulgated in 2010. The Framework Act defines the missions, goals, and principles of ODA. Article 3 of the Framework Act identifies the basic principles of international development cooperation as: (i) reduce poverty in developing countries; (ii) improve the human rights of women and children and achieve gender equality; (iii) realize sustainable development and humanitarianism; (iv) promote cooperative economic relations with developing partners; and (v) pursue peace and prosperity in the international community.

Prior to the initiatives of the current Moon administration, South Korea had launched three major ODA platforms. First, the Knowledge Sharing Program (KSP) was launched in 2004 and advertised as a "new paradigm of development cooperation" and a "knowledge-intensive development and economic cooperation program designed to share Korea's development experience with partner countries" (KSP 2013). Second, the Development Experience Exchange Program (DEEP), run by KOICA, based on knowledge transfer of South Korean expertise and experience (including two decades of KOICA ODA activities), looks to provide a dynamic transition model tailored to the specific needs of individual development partners and their operating environments (Lee, S. 2014, 18). Third, the World Friends Korea volunteer organization seeks "to improve the quality of life of residents in developing countries; to increase cooperation and mutual understanding between developing countries and South Korea; [and] to achieve self-realization and growth through service activities" (World Friends Korea 2016). The ROK is one of only six countries that has such an overseas volunteer program (the others are Belgium, Germany, Japan, Luxembourg, and the United States), and South Korea's program is second only to the United States' in terms of size (Roehrig 2013, 632).

In recent years, the most prominent of these initiatives has been the "Global Korea" agenda pursued by the Lee Myung-bak administration (2008–2013), the aims of which included being "a global actor with broad horizons that engages proactively with the international community in the service of peace and development in the world" and a state which "should seek the attributes of a soft, strong power as it builds up its capacities to become a global actor" (Office of the President 2009, 12–13). Olbrich and Shim (2012, 2) see the Global Korea strategy as embodying "South Korea's global ambitions in development and security" as well as bolstering international influence and reputation. Kalinowski and Cho (2012, 243) have noted how under the guise of the Global Korea strategy the Lee Myung-bak administration further prioritized the economic realm in South Korean foreign policy, with South Korea seeking to turn its economic success story into a political asset and using its increasing economic clout to expand into global politics in order to protect and facilitate its economic interests abroad. This policy had a significant pre-history, however, in the resource diplomacy of the preceding liberal Roh Moo-hyun administration (2003–2008).

Thus, the central role of economic development in South Korean international policy-making is an area of remarkable consensus.

According to Watson (2013, 234), "for the South Korean government, by linking its foreign aid with South Korean corporations, the activities reflect the soft power of the government as 'national brand.'" Likewise, for *The Economist* (2012), while interest in the South Korean model of economic success has been around for a while, "what has changed in recent years is the government's willingness to promote the success and the increasing number of newly developing countries that want to learn from it." Both Brand Korea and attempts by the ROK government to promote it are in fact multi-faceted. The Presidential Council on Nation Branding (PCNB) has in fact set out five priority areas aimed at proactively transitioning Korea away from its perceived periphery image within global society and, in combination with "contribution diplomacy," "aims to promote Seoul's leadership in tackling global issues such as climate change and poverty reduction through its ODA" (Kim 2011, 810).

President Moon Jae-in was inaugurated in 2017. He has shown interest in expanding the volume of ODA, because South Korea's ODA/GNI ratio in 2016, at 0.14 percent, was one of the lowest among OECD countries. He also argued that ODA should be aligned with migration, climate change, human rights, and governance (Yonhap News 2017). President Moon announced the New Southern Policy in November 2017 during his visit to three ASEAN countries, Vietnam, Indonesia, and the Philippines, to enhance South Korea's strategic ties with nations in Southeast Asia. The New Southern Policy is a part of President Moon's "Northeast Asia Plus Community of Responsibility," which is a multi-directional diplomatic set of initiatives including the New Northern Policy (China, Russia), the New Western Policy (Europe), and the New Southern Policy (ASEAN, Australia, New Zealand, India). While previous administrations focused on Northeast Asia or Asia in general, this is the first attempt specifically to place ASEAN at the forefront of policy agenda since the former President Kim Dae-jung's administration (1998–2003).

Historically, South Korea's diplomacy and foreign policy have disproportionately focused on North Korea, the US, and China due to the security challenges on the Korean peninsula. By diversifying and expanding the diplomatic and economic relations, South Korea seeks to create new strategic regions (Lee 2017). President Moon explained his "3P" plan of the New Southern Policy as people-centered, peace-loving, and mutually prosperous community, along with his economic and sociocultural initiatives. Rather than considering ASEAN as a market for South Korean exports, it is to achieve mutual growth through economic cooperation and eventually to achieve peace. In particular, it is important to note that this plan includes cooperation in nontraditional security areas such as anti-terrorism, food security, and energy security (Kang 2018).

President Moon nominated Kang Kyung-wha as the Minister of Ministry of Foreign Affairs (MOFA) in 2017. Minister Kang has held several positions at the UN including Deputy High Commissioner for Human Rights and Assistant Secretary-General for the Office for the Coordination of Humanitarian Affairs. In May 2017, Minister Kang emphasized the importance of humanitarian assistance in North Korea despite the continuing provocations from Pyongyang, and said that "humanitarian aid is a universal human value that we must undertake when people are suffering, and it should be addressed separately from political considerations. . . . That is the UN's principle" (Hankyoreh News 2017). Hence, the major policy actors, instruments, and statements of the Moon administration have, thus far, looked to tie development assistance ever more closely to the humanitarian focus identified in this volume as being a key aspect of niche diplomacy by these middle powers. These statements also link to the next section on human security promotion.

At this stage, however, it is important to consider a number of caveats regarding South Korean international assistance and the reception it receives internationally in terms of serving as a useful area of niche diplomacy. For a start, it is far from certain that South Korea's ODA recipient experience can or should be replicated. The first period of development assistance to South Korea was boosted by the presence of an occupying power that provided most of the grants. The second was characterized primarily by grants and unconditional ODA, the relative absence of which in South Korea's own assistance programs has led to international criticism. The third depended not only on reparations from the former colonial power, but also from the tremendous boost the South Korean economy received from US involvement in wars in Southeast Asia. The fourth saw political transformation and consolidation as a democracy, but also as the foundation of future governance challenges. The fifth witnessed ongoing economic transformation, including the weathering of the Asian financial crises and the adoption of International Monetary Fund (IMF) prescriptions with regard to market opening and neoliberal reforms, all of which have posed additional challenges to the well-being of vulnerable groups in the ROK.

The South Korean emphasis on education in the country's own development and in its knowledge sharing and ODA is also potentially problematic. Education has always held a privileged position in South Korean society. Other societies may not be able to manufacture such dedication to and respect for education. Furthermore, there have been some negative impacts of this focus in the ROK. The concentration of public and private funds on education leaves less for other human needs. There is an inflation of academic qualifications, while a scarcity of practical skills. Finally, educational competition has increased the strain on society, on students, on families, and on academics. Even the overt use of the term "Korean Model of Development" has been criticized as implying "'one size fits all' – a singular mode of development – which does not fit with the global norms on foreign aid and development cooperation that recognize diverse developmental contexts of recipient nations" (Kim, Kim, and Kim 2013, 315). By placing an emphasis on the Korean model, there is a risk that Seoul's policies will be viewed as self-centered and derived from overconfidence in the country's own development success, and it might be "received as arrogance unless carefully executed" (Chun, Munyi, and Lee 2010, 799).

South Korea has been further criticized not only for its relatively low level of ODA as a proportion of gross domestic product (GDP), but also for high levels of tied aid. South Korean aid topped only US$500 million in the mid-2000s, and although it reached US$1.325 billion in 2011, this was only equivalent to 0.12 percent of its GNI (OECD 2012). South Korea's ODA volume in 2011 was 6 percent greater than in 2010, but when its aid surpassed US$1 billion for the first time, its ODA/GNI ratio was unchanged from 2010 and below DAC members' average of 0.32 percent as well as its target of 0.13 percent for the year. South Korea committed to increase the total volume of ODA to about US$3 billion and ODA/GNI to 0.25 percent by 2015, but this has not been achieved. South Korea's total volume of ODA and its ODA/GNI ratio remain relatively small when compared with other traditional donor countries in North America, Western Europe, and, in particular, the Nordic countries. Indeed, South Korea has been ranked at or near the bottom of many quantitative measurements of ODA of DAC member countries. These include total ODA, ODA/GNI ratio, bilateral aid/ODA ratio, grants/ODA ratio, humanitarian grants/ODA ratio, multilateral aid/ODA ratio, and the Commitment to Development Index, comprising the seven areas of aid, trade, investment, technology, environment, migration, and security (Choi 2010, 42; Lee, A. 2014, 41; Lee, S. 2014, 17; Park 2014, 2).

Historically, much of South Korea's aid has been tied, or given on condition that it be spent on goods or services provided by the South Korean interests. In 2006, as much as 98 percent of the ROK's aid was estimated as being tied or partially tied (Kalinowski and Cho 2012, 249). In 2007, some progress appeared to have been made, with as much as 25 percent of South Korean aid being untied, but this was still well below the OECD DAC member average (Park 2010). Consequently, as "part of its accession to the DAC and its commitment to the Paris Declaration principles and the Accra Agenda for Action, in 2009 South Korea put a timetable in place to increase the untied portion of its bilateral ODA to 75 percent by 2015" (OECD 2012, 20). By the time of the OECD DAC peer review in 2012, however, it was noted that South Korea had in fact made no progress toward this aim, but rather, "the untied proportion of South Korea's total aid was lower in 2010 (at 32 percent) than in 2009 (44 percent)" (*ibid.*).

Nevertheless, South Korea remains committed to ODA, perhaps, at least in part, because it meshes with the pursuit of the country's own national interest. Furthermore, humanitarian considerations are playing an increased role in Seoul's strategic deliberations, as will be developed further in the next section.

South Korea's human security promotion

In the security field, due to geopolitical constraints, the ROK is unable to perform the neutral or brokering role of traditional middle powers (Kalinowski and Cho 2012, 244). Thus, Seoul's major policy forays and initiatives in the security realm have tended to revolve around the intersection of security and development, and how this intersection contributes to peacebuilding. Again, Seoul's bilateral policy-making in this area has had, at most, limited success. These include approaches to North Korea, such as the Kaesong Industrial Complex (KIC), the "Sunshine Policy" of the Kim Dae-jung administration, and elements of the "Trustpolitik" initiated during the Park Geun-hye administration (2013–2017). All of these initiatives were subject to politicization by the actors, and ultimately did little to build trust, let alone contribute to peacebuilding. Bilateral initiatives in the traditional security realm are too obviously strategic in terms of attempting, first and foremost, to promote national interest of the ROK. Emphasizing the need for Korean unification as a prerequisite for peace in the region would seem to be a case of putting the cart before the horse. Yet Korean policy focusing on nontraditional security (NTS) aims, and those related to multilateralism, have had greater success.

It is important to note that the South Korean government has not explicitly used the term "human security" in most of its documents and ODA projects. Elements of human security have, nonetheless, suffused Korea's foreign policy. The first official occurrence of the term "human security" in Korean government documentation was in 2008 when it was used by MOFA. The term was used in broader discussions on foreign policy without an explicit focus on ODA. MOFA and KOICA were the only two government institutions that used "human security" in their official documents, but again, that was only in the reference section explaining ODA terminology.

MOFA stated that human security has become very important since we are faced with nontraditional security threats including terrorism, environmental degradation, transnational crimes, internal conflict, poverty, and disasters, and further defined the concept of human security as follows: "Individual security and safety, protection of human rights, and protection of individual's basic necessities" (MOFA 2008). Protection of individual safety and human dignity were seen as important for international peace and security. Thus, the government affirms the basic goals of human security and the international community's emphasis on human security and common value of humanism. MOFA stated that "there is a need to cooperate at the regional and global levels to deal with traditional as well as non-traditional security threats" (*ibid.*). This is in line with the freedom from fear component of human security.

President Park Geun-hye used the term during her presidential campaign speech on foreign policy, national security, and unification (November 5, 2012): "I will promote sustainable development and enduring peace in Northeast Asia. I will cooperate with all nations interested in this vision in building trust, cooperation in national security, social and economic relations, and human security" (News 1 2012). Likewise, former Foreign Minister Yun Byung-se used "human security" at an international conference in 2013 on the theme "New Strategic Thinking: Planning for Korean Foreign Policy." This was the first time a Minster of Foreign Affairs had used the term. He stated that the global policies of the Park Administration "reflect the belief that peace and prosperity of South Korea and the world are indivisible, and that there has been a global paradigm shift which emphasizes the importance of human security" (MOFA 2013).

Although the South Korean government rarely uses the term "human security" in its official documents, it has embraced the concept and its implications for ethical foreign policy fully. For example, MOFA affirms the goals for ODA as economic development and poverty reduction of developing countries (MOFA 2018a), and commitments based on humanitarianism and sustainable development (MOFA 2018b). South Korea has endorsed international humanitarian assistance for the protection of basic human rights of people and freedom from fear (MOFA 2018c). The first paragraph of Article 3 of the Framework Act highlights reduction of poverty; human rights of women, children, and the handicapped, and gender equality; and sustainable development, humanitarianism, and peace (MOFA 2018d). MOFA included "strengthening of humanitarian assistance and peacebuilding effort for the regions in conflict" in the six strategic goals of its ODA. It aimed to gradually increase ODA for human security and humanitarian assistance.

The government has promulgated the Overseas Emergency Relief Act (2014) and the Strategic Plan for International Development Cooperation (2010). The government embraces both the protection and empowerment approaches in humanitarian assistance and tries to link short-term humanitarian assistance and long-term reconstruction efforts in line with disaster risk reduction (DRR). MOFA announced "the Strategic Plan for International Humanitarian Assistance" (May 2010) and "the Strategic Plan for International Development Cooperation" (October 2010). In addition, it expanded the emergency relief budget and trained and dispatched humanitarian assistance professionals in humanitarian crises. These efforts reflected the government's effort to expand international humanitarian assistance and improve overseas emergency relief system (MOFA 2018e). MOFA's Overseas Emergency Relief Act 2014 details the law and implementation guidelines for international humanitarian assistance (*ibid.*).

The South Korean government's Mid-Term ODA Policy for 2011–2015 presents policy directions and annual ODA target, ODA allocation guidelines by region and by income group, and partnership strategy with major developing countries. It includes plans to distribute 40 percent of grants to the least developed countries (LDCs) and fragile states and 30 percent to countries in conflict (PMO 2010a). The government aims to provide humanitarian assistance in disaster-affected areas, reflecting the freedom from fear (PMO 2010b). It aims to reduce poverty and improve the quality of life in developing countries, which is the freedom to live in dignity (*ibid.*, 52). Bringing hope to recipient countries and emphasizing poverty eradication and self-help reflect the freedom from want and empowerment (PMO 2010b). More recently, the Mid-Term ODA Policy for 2016–2020 presented new ODA targets: to increase its ODA/GNI to 0.20 percent by 2020 and to the DAC average of 0.30 percent by 2030 (ODA Korea 2016). It increases assistance to social and economic infrastructure, health, education, and cross-cutting areas (environment), and humanitarian assistance. In addition, it clearly stated South Korea's intention of contributing to global poverty alleviation and sustainable development, and aspirations to contribute to the co-prosperity of humanity and global peace.

The Prime Minister's Office (PMO) published the first ODA White Paper in 2014. It reviewed the policy and practice on humanitarian assistance and fragile states (PMO 2010b). The ODA White Paper shows that South Korea's ODA aims to reduce poverty in developing countries and promote sustainable development based on humanitarianism. It aims to improve the human rights of women, children, and the handicapped, as well as gender equality in developing countries as stated in Article 3 (*ibid.*, 52). Emphasis on economic development and human rights refers to the approach to freedom from want and freedom to live in dignity. South Korea's ODA includes infrastructure for development, improvement of relations with developing countries, and solutions for global problems. The recent ODA White Paper in 2017 emphasized South Korea's transparency and accountability in development cooperation. Thus, the South Korean government is committed to upgrading its ODA in line with its new strategic pillars (effective

ODA, transparent ODA, and collaborative ODA) (*ibid.*, 5). South Korea also expanded its efforts to assist fragile states in the name of peacebuilding, humanitarian assistance, and development cooperation.

South Korea's humanitarian policies are based on the four principles of humanity, neutrality, impartiality, and independence. Humanitarian assistance in South Korea is defined as an intervention to help people who are victims of a natural disaster or conflict to meet their basic needs and rights (KDR 2018b). The South Korean government works closely with civil society organizations in particular before implementing humanitarian interventions in fragile states where armed conflicts have caused severe damage (KDR 2018b). Civil society representatives urge the government to make sure that international humanitarian assistance is in accordance with international humanitarian laws and norms.

Based on humanitarianism, South Korea considers the requests of the government in damaged countries and the international economic status of South Korea when providing overseas emergency relief (KOICA 2012). South Korea will work closely with recipient countries or international organizations to carry out the urgent international humanitarian assistance. Southeast Asia, the ROK's "near abroad," has been a major focus of Korean soft power and public diplomacy initiatives. South Korea has consistently concentrated 30 percent of its total ODA to members of the ASEAN. The ASEAN-ROK Cooperation Fund, established in 1990, expended almost US$67 million through the end of 2014, and operates (from 2015) with an annual budget of US$7 million, funding developmental projects dealing with technology transfer, human resource development, people-to-people exchanges, and exchanges of intellectuals between Korea and ASEAN (ASEAN-ROK 2018). The five least developed ASEAN countries (which therefore have the greatest human security and development challenges, and the most to gain from partnering with South Korea) are the Philippines and the CLMV countries.

Since 1990, the Philippines has been one of Korea's prioritized partner countries for ODA with the focused aims of poverty reduction and economic development, especially in the areas of rural development, education, infrastructure, health, and environment. Korea has also started to turn its attention to humanitarian or principled diplomatic and development engagement in the CLMV region. Each of these four countries is conflict-affected, and given the even higher prevalence of poverty, has perhaps greater need for Korean assistance. As part of its efforts, South Korea has made good progress toward ensuring better humanitarian donorship through a legislative framework for its humanitarian action and a commitment to increase its humanitarian aid.

According to the basic policy on international humanitarian assistance, the South Korean government prioritizes the country that cannot address emergency disasters themselves or that needs immediate support (KOICA 2012). In March 2007, South Korea enacted the Overseas Emergency Relief Act designed to allow the Korean government to provide more effective and prompter overseas emergency relief in order to play a greater role in the concerted efforts of the global community toward disaster management (subsequently updated, amended, and reenacted in 2010, 2011, 2014, and 2017). This has been followed by the Policy Framework on Overseas Emergency Relief (September 2015) and Humanitarian Assistance Strategy (March 2015). The ROK has been part of the UN Disaster Assessment and Coordination (UNDAC) teams since 2003 and the International Search and Rescue Advisory Group (INSARAG) since 1999. Since South Korea specializes in search and rescue efforts, it has participated in the OCHA-administered Asia Pacific Humanitarian Partnership (APHP) since its establishment in 2004. It has provided international humanitarian assistance to many countries including the Philippines and the CLMV countries.

South Korea provided the largest contingent of forces for relief and reconstruction efforts in the Philippines after the devastation wrought by Typhoon Haiyan in November 2013. Furthermore, the ROK forces were committed to the mission for far longer than those of any other contributing nation – two full six-month tours of duty rather than just helping with the emergency relief mission in the immediate aftermath of the disaster (Arcala Hall 2016). In November 2013, the South Korean government sent US$100,000 to Cambodia for restoring the flood damage (KDR 2018a). South Korea also provided humanitarian assistance to Myanmar from January to June in 2015, in particular to the refugees fleeing from the civil war, with tents and settlements (KDR 2018a). The South Korean government has also provided assistance in the health sector. In August 2013, South Korea sent US$200,000 to Laos for eradication of dengue (KDR 2018a). And in Vietnam, South Korean officials visited the flood-damaged areas to check the status in order to provide the most necessary immediate assistance to Vietnam from October 2013 to January 2014 (KDR 2018a).

Thus, the ROK has increasingly prioritized initiatives promoting humanitarian goals and human security, substantially to the benefit of vulnerable individuals and groups in Southeast Asia, but also to its own benefit, as such initiatives are considered a key element of Korea's public diplomacy. Yet, again, some caveats must be recognized in terms of South Korea's role, policies, and impact in these areas. At the official launch of the ROK's new Act on Public Diplomacy in August 2016, the old, soft power interpretations of public diplomacy and middle-powerism remained in the fore. For instance, Duk-min Yun, Chancellor of the Korea National Diplomatic Academy, claimed that "now is the time for Korea's public diplomacy to take a leap forward, given the significance of soft power in determining a middle power's diplomatic sway" (Shin 2016). An official emphasis on soft power, winning hearts and minds, and promoting unification means that there is a danger that ROK initiatives will be written off as spin, or worse, as propaganda or even as hostile intervention. One irony of soft power is that "the theory emphasizes the importance of attraction in world affairs but presents that attraction as a mechanism for getting one's way, which is potentially an unattractive objective" (Cull 2006). Our final analytical section, therefore, assesses South Korea's engagement with contemporary, multilateral definitions of what it is to be a successful middle power.

Analysis of South Korea as a middle power

"Middle power states have most recently been defined by their internationalism. States that exhibit certain foreign policy behavior are considered middle powers. Qualifying behavior might include good 'global citizenship,' niche diplomacy, and accepting roles as mediators, followers, or staunch multilateralists" (Rudderham 2008, 2). From this perspective, status as a middle power is conferred in accordance with behavior rather than size. Middle power activism is all about visibility on the international stage, but it is also about playing by the rules of the global normative consensus and demonstrating a willingness to be a good global citizen. Although not as developed an area of South Korean policy-making, collaborative middle power activism perhaps holds even greater promise of benefit to both the ROK and to other countries.

South Korea does already play an active role in multilateral UN human security mechanisms such as the Office for the Coordination of Humanitarian Affairs (OCHA), which is the main UN body designed to strengthen the UN's response to both complex emergencies and natural disasters. The ROK government has also officially expressed its support for the responsibility to protect (R2P) principles. These roles and policies not only reflect an alternative strategic mission for the ROK, but also spill over into the realm of global governance and good international citizenship. The ROK supports all internationally agreed-upon humanitarian principles such as impartiality, neutrality, and independence, and applies them to foreign, security, and assistance policies.

MOFA affirmed its implementation of the UN Security Council Resolution 1325 on Women, Peace, and Security, and emphasized empowering women in conflict prevention, conflict resolution, and peacebuilding (MOFA 2018e). MOFA's documents show a strong interest in human security, although the term was not used explicitly. It has raised the effectiveness of humanitarian assistance by working closely with international humanitarian organizations and consultative groups. Finally, MOFA has expanded its

role in response to international humanitarian crises through active participation with UNDP, World Food Programme (WFP), UN Children's Fund
(UNICEF), and International Committee of the Red Cross (ICRC).

The most visible contribution as a good global citizen, and one closely
linked with peacebuilding, has come in the ROK involvement in peacekeeping and other UN missions. Despite a heavy emphasis on the promotion of national interest in South Korean international policy-making,
nevertheless, one area in which normative considerations do structure
ROK international policy formation is through what has become known
as the "paying back syndrome," wherein South Koreans believe that it is
their "moral duty to help those who are caught in armed conflict" in return
for the international assistance the country received during the Korean
War (Hong 2009, 24). Such sentiments were also expressed by Sung Joo
Han, former minister of Foreign Affairs, and Min Koo Han, former Minister of National Defense at a recent conference on international peacekeeping (Han 2014b, 2014a).

"Paying back" also of course applies to government and public support
for increasing South Korean ODA. Iain Watson (2013, 224–5) has identified
"a national consensus that crosses party lines and which is often based on
South Korean exceptionalism and patriotism . . . broken down into Seoul
'paying back' those countries that had helped Korea" with domestic public
support for ODA linked to a "South Korean sense of honour, fairness and
justice to foreigners." While the concept may be more prevalent among
policy elites and older generations, and rather abstract for the youth, nevertheless, there remains a strong impetus for humanitarian participation and
activism among young South Koreans, as has been demonstrated in high
levels of domestic and international volunteerism (Howe 2014, 56–8), as
well as participation in protests.

The ROK acceded to membership of the UN in 1991 and has grown
from being the host of the largest UN enforcement operation to date, to
being a major contributor to international peacekeeping operations. For
Eun-Sook Chung (2010, 101), Seoul's support for UN PKOs "conveys the
message of reciprocating international assistance it received after 1945,
and it also demonstrates the nation's will and capabilities to contribute to
the maintenance of peace in the international community." Furthermore,
for Sangtu Ko (2012, 288), peacekeeping operations represent the one
field where Korea truly aspires to middle power activism. While still modest, Korea's troop contributions are already substantial when compared
with other medium-size country members of the OECD such as Japan, the
United Kingdom, or Germany. Currently, the ROK ranks 39th in military
and police contributors to UN operations, with just over 600 currently
active personnel (UN 2015).

Furthermore, senior political and military leaders have repeatedly iterated the intent to expand the ROK's role. President Lee Myung-bak stated in 2009, at an event commemorating national independence, that he would "raise the value of the national brand through optimal use of two instruments, namely ODA and PKO" (Ko 2012, 296). The 2010 Defense White Paper announced a plan steadily to expand South Korea's participation in international peace-keeping operations. In July 2013, the Joint Chiefs of Staff talked of further beefing up South Korea's presence in international PKOs (Kang 2013). Also, in 2013, in order to improve the functioning of South Korean peacekeeping operations, the government increased the staff of the PKO Center and relocated it from the ROK Joint Staff College to the National Defense University. The PKO center provides pre-deployment education and training to military and police personnel, writes up the "after action" reports to assess the effectiveness of the unit, and gathers any lessons learned for future missions, while also participating in exchange programs with PKO units from other countries to improve training and coordination (Roehrig 2013, 639). These aspirations have started to be reflected in practice.

South Korea's growing ODA to developing countries and interest in human security show signs that South Korea is pursuing its middle-powerism through these activities. The extent of the impact of South Korea's middle-powerism in the region and the world is yet to be determined, however. At the very least, we can say that these policy arenas hold great promise for Korea's niche diplomacy, that the ROK government is increasingly committed to them, and that collaborative action by middle powers (including, potentially, between South Korea and Japan) is starting to be recognized by policymakers as the best way forward. With the recent South Korea–North Korea Summit in April 2018 and US–North Korea Summit in June 2018, we have also begun to witness an expanding role for South Korea in regional and global security discussions. The role of South Korea in these events and in subsequent peace efforts on the Korean peninsula signals growing promise for role of South Korea as an influential "middle power" in peace-building as well.

Note

1 This paper is drawn substantially from Eun Mee Kim, Seon Young Bae, and Ji Hyun Shin (2018), "Human Security in Practice: The Case of South Korea"; and Brendan Howe (2018), "Korea's Role for Peacebuilding and Development in Asia." Major sections of the above two papers have been used verbatim or have been paraphrased. Eun Mee Kim gratefully acknowledges research support provided by Soo Young Kim and Yoorim Bang of the Graduate School of International Studies of Ewha Womans University. Corresponding author: Eun Mee Kim (emkim@ewha.ac.kr).

References

Arcala Hall, R. (2016) Interviewed by Howe, B. in Seoul, May 30.

ASEAN-ROK (2018) *ASEAN-ROK Cooperation Fund* (http://overseas.mofa.go.kr/asean-en/wpge/m_2573/contents.do) Accessed July 20, 2018.

Choi, J. (2010) "From a recipient to a donor state: Achievements and challenges of Korea's ODA" *International Review of Public Administration* 15(3) 37–51.

Chun, H., Munyi, E., and Lee, H. (2010) "South Korea as an emerging donor: Challenges and changes on its entering OECD/DAC" *Journal of International Development* 22(6) 788–802.

Chung, E. (2010) "Korea's Law on UNPKO and its role in international peacekeeping missions" *Korea Focus* 18(2) 98–102.

Cull, N. (2006) "'Public diplomacy' before Gullion: The evolution of a phrase" *USC Center on Public Diplomacy (CPD) Blog* April 18 (http://uscpublicdiplomacy.org/blog/060418_public_diplomacy_before_gullion_the_evolution_of_a_phrase) Accessed July 20, 2018.

The Economist (2012) "South Korea's influence in Asia: This year's model" February 18 (www.economist.com/node/21547865) Accessed July 20, 2018.

Han, M. (2014a) *Keynote Speech at the PKO International Conference: New Challenges and Future Prospects of Peacekeeping Operations* November 13 Sookmyung Women's University, Seoul.

Han, S. (2014b) *Congratulatory Remarks at the PKO International Conference: New Challenges and Future Prospects of Peacekeeping Operations* November 13 Sookmyung Women's University, Seoul.

Hankyoreh News (2017) "Minister of Foreign Affairs nominee says 'stiffer sanctions' needed on North Korea" *Hankyoreh* May 26 (http://english.hani.co.kr/arti/english_edition/e_national/796392.html) Accessed July 20, 2018.

Hong, K. (2009) "South Korean approaches to peacekeeping and peacebuilding: Lessons learned and challenges ahead" *The Journal of East Asian Affairs* 23(1) 23–45.

Howe, B. ed. (2014) *Korea in the World: Promoting Mutual Understanding and Global Partnerships* Ministry of Foreign Affairs, Seoul.

Kalinowski, T. and Cho, H. (2012) "Korea's search for a global role between hard economic interests and soft power" *European Journal of Development Research* 24 242–60.

Kang, M. (2018) "Economic and diplomatic significance of New Southern Policy" *KDB Industrial Bank Issue Analysis* 748 64–75.

Kang, S. (2013) "Korea beefing up presence in PKO" *The Korea Times* July 11 (www.koreatimes.co.kr/www/news/nation/2013/07/116_139642.html) Accessed July 20, 2018.

Kim, E. M. (1997) *Big Business, Strong State: Collusion and Conflict in South Korean Development, 1960–1990* State University of New York Press, New York.

Kim, E. M., Bae, S. Y., and Shin, J. H. (2018) "Human security in practice: The case of South Korea," in Mine, Yoichi, Oscar A. Gomez, and Ako Muto, eds., *Human Security Norms in East Asia*. Basingstoke, UK: Palgrave Macmillan.

Kim, E. M., Kim, P. H., and Kim, J. (2013) "From development to development cooperation: Foreign aid, country ownership, and the developmental state in South Korea" *The Pacific Review* 26(3) 313–36.

Kim, S. (2011) "Bridging troubled worlds? An analysis of the ethical case for South Korean aid" *Journal of International Development* 23 802–22.

Knowledge Sharing Program (KSP) (2013) "Policy consultation: Bilateral KSP" (www.ksp.go.kr/pillars/policymain.jsp) Accessed July 20, 2018.

Ko, S. (2012) "Korea's middle power activism and peacekeeping operations" *Asia Europe Journal* 10 287–99.

Korea Disaster Relief (KDR) (2018a) "The current status of humanitarian assistance" (http://humanitarian.koica.go.kr/c3/sub1.do) Accessed July 20, 2018.

———— (2018b) "The four principles of humanitarian assistance" (http://humanitarian.koica.go.kr/c1/sub2.jsp) Accessed July 20, 2018.

Korea International Cooperation Agency (KOICA) (2012) "Research on humanitarian assistance policy and projects: With a focus on emergency relief system" (www.oda.go.kr/opo/cmcd/comm/downloadFile.do?P_STRE_FILE_NM=kms 8988371914651032789.pdf) Accessed July 20, 2018.

Lee, A. (2014) "Post-Busan and new paradigm for international development cooperation" *Workshop on Economic Development Policy for Government Officials of Nepal* July 22 Korea Development Institute (KDI) School, Seoul (www.kdevelopedia.org/resource/view/04201408040133449.do#.VKkiZeamqpo) Accessed July 27, 2018.

Lee, J. (2017) "Korea's new Southern policy towards ASEAN: Context and direction" *Jeju Peace Institute International Symposium: Northeast Asia Plus Community of Responsibility* July 15 Jeju Peace Institute, Seogwipo (http://jpi.or.kr/skyboard/download.sky?fid=4975&gid=7073&code=jpiworld) Accessed July 25, 2018.

Lee, S. (2014) "Multilayered world order and South Korea's middle power diplomacy: The case of development cooperation policy" *EAI MPDI Working Paper* October (www.eai.or.kr/data/bbs/eng_report/2014102816225492.pdf) Accessed July 27, 2018.

Ministry of Foreign Affairs (MOFA) (2008) "The South Korean government's views on human security".

———— (2013) "Yun Byung-se, opening remarks at the new strategic thinking: Planning for Korean foreign policy" April 26 (www.mofa.go.kr/www/brd/m_20140/view.do?seq=301856&srchFr=&srchTo=&srchWord=&srchTp=&multi_itm_seq=0&itm_seq_1=0&itm_seq_2=0&company_cd=&company_nm=&page=25) Accessed July 20, 2018.

———— (2018a) "Development cooperation" (www.mofa.go.kr/www/wpge/m_3816/contents.do) Accessed July 20, 2018.

———— (2018b) "ODA propelling system and support status" (www.mofa.go.kr/www/wpge/m_3840/contents.do) Accessed July 20, 2018.

———— (2018c) "Policy direction of South Korea's development cooperation" (www.mofa.go.kr/www/wpge/m_3839/contents.do) Accessed July 20, 2018.

———— (2018d) "The framework act on international development cooperation" (www.law.go.kr/lsInfoP.do?lsiSeq=142005&efYd=20140101#0000) Accessed July 20, 2018.

———— (2018e) "Overseas emergency relief" (www.mofa.go.kr/www/wpge/m_3839/contents.do) Accessed July 20, 2018.

News 1 (2012) "Park Geun-hye, Presidential Candidate of the Saenuri Party, Park's Policies on Foreign Policy, National Security and Unification" *News1* November 5 (http://news1.kr/articles/?880552) Accessed July 20, 2018.

ODA Korea (2014) "Korea's ODA White Paper: Opening a new era of happiness for all humanity" (www.odakorea.go.kr/hz.blltn.pnrSl.do?bltn_seq=5&sys_cd=&brd_seq=22&targetRow=&blltn_div=oda&keyword_top=&searchKey=01&keyword) Accessed July 20, 2018.

――― (2016) "Mid-term strategy for development cooperation 2016–2020" (www.odakorea.go.kr/eng.policy.Mid-termODAPolicy.do) Accessed July 20, 2018.

――― (2018) "History of Korea's ODA" (www.odakorea.go.kr/eng.overview.History.do) Accessed July 20, 2018.

Office of the President (2009) *Global Korea: The National Security Strategy of the Republic of Korea* Cheong Wa Dae, Seoul.

Olbrich, P. and Shim, D. (2012) "South Korea as a global actor: International contributions to development and security" *German Institute of Global and Area Studies (GIGA) Focus No. 2* (www.giga-hamburg.de/en/system/files/publications/gf_international_1202.pdf) Accessed July 20, 2018.

Organisation for Economic Cooperation and Development (OECD) (2012) "Korea: Development Assistance Committee (DAC) peer review 2012" (www.oecd.org/dac/peer-reviews/Korea%20CRC%20-%20FINAL%2021%20JAN.pdf) Accessed July 20, 2018.

Park, K. H. (2010) "Korea's role in global development" *Brookings East Asia Commentary No. 36* February (www.brookings.edu/research/opinions/2010/02/09-korea-global-development) Accessed July 20, 2018.

Park, S. (2014) "South Korea and the European Union: A promising partnership for development cooperation?" *European Strategic Partnerships Observatory Policy Brief No. 15* November (http://fride.org/download/PB_15_South_Korea_and_the_European_Union.pdf) Accessed July 20, 2018.

Prime Minister's Office (PMO) (2010a) "Mid-term ODA policy for 2011–2015" (http://odakorea.go.kr/ODAPage_2012/T02/L01_S04.jsp) Accessed July 20, 2018.

――― (2010b) "Strategic plan for international development cooperation" (http://odakorea.go.kr/hz.blltn.PolicySl.do?bltn_seq=105&sys_cd=&brd_seq=9&targetRow=31&blltn_div=oda&searchKey=01&keyword) Accessed July 20, 2018.

Roehrig, T. (2013) "South Korea, foreign aid, and UN peacekeeping: Contributing to international peace and security as a middle power" *Korea Observer* 44(4) 623–45.

Rudderham, M. A. (2008) "Middle power pull: Can middle powers use public diplomacy to ameliorate the image of the West?" *YCISS Working Paper No. 46* (http://yciss.info.yorku.ca/files/2012/06/WP46-Rudderham.pdf) Accessed July 20, 2018.

Shin, H. H. (2016) "New law to boost public diplomacy" *Korea Herald* August 4 (www.koreaherald.com/view.php?ud=20160804000679) Accessed July 27, 2018.

Stallings, B. and Kim, E. M. (2017) *Promoting Development: The Political Economy of East Asian Foreign Aid* Palgrave Macmillan, London.

United Nations (UN) (2015) "Ranking of military and police contributions to UN operations" (www.un.org/en/peacekeeping/contributors/2015/mar15_2.pdf) Accessed July 20, 2018.

Watson, I. (2013) "Beyond the aid trap for emerging donors: Private and public partnerships in South Korea's Official Development Assistance (ODA) strategy" *Journal of Comparative Asian Development* 12(2) 212–44.

World Friends Korea (2016) "The footsteps of world friends Korea" (www.worldfriendskorea.or.kr/eng/historyInfo/eng.intro.history/list.do) Accessed July 20, 2018.

Yonhap News (2017) "Moon Jae-in, utilizing ODA as a representative diplomatic brand" *Yonhap News* May 10 (www.yonhapnews.co.kr/bulletin/2017/05/10/0200 000000AKR20170510076400371.HTML) Accessed July 20, 2018.

6 Summaries and prescriptions

Brendan Howe

Two middle powers

What the preceding chapters have demonstrated is not only that Japan and South Korea are middle powers, but also that they are a special type of middle power, with shared constraints and similar rational imperatives propelling the construction of their niche diplomacy. They of course share the geographic location and geostrategic constraints of the Northeast Asian operating environment. All four of the other powers in the region, the United States (US), the People's Republic of China (PRC), Russia, and the Democratic People's Republic of Korea (DPRK) are now nuclear armed powers, a criterion which by some measurements forms the dividing line between great powers and the rest. Three of them, the US, PRC, and Russia, also command much greater traditional power resources than either Japan or the Republic of Korea (ROK) are able to muster. Furthermore, Japan is (at least currently) constrained by the strictures of its "pacifist constitution," and is considered by some commentators to be so deferential to the US with regard to traditional diplomacy and security considerations as to be regarded as a "reactive state" (Calder 1988; Hirata 1998). At the same time, South Korea is so closely tied to the US in traditional security terms that it has yet to regain operational control (OPCON) of its own armed forced in times of war (although President Moon has recently made this a priority), and only gained control of them during peacetime in 1994 (Frances 2017). The threats posed by an antagonistic North Korea and also a rising China have also been a major preoccupation for both Tokyo and Seoul, making the two countries keen, albeit junior, partners in their respective military alliances with the US.

Thus, for both Japan and South Korea, concentrating limited national resources as niche diplomatic output in traditional security arenas is not really an option. As middle powers, they have had, therefore, to look elsewhere to get more bang for their bucks, yen, or won. The evolving international operating environment, reflecting extensive penetration of the products of the communication and information technology revolution, combined with the universalization of normative humanitarian imperatives, has created an opportunity for both countries to exert international influence in fields related to nontraditional and human security. In particular, the use of development assistance to facilitate the construction of safe havens free from fear, want, and indignity, has become characteristic of the aid platforms of both Tokyo and Seoul. This niche diplomatic output has also experienced a geographic refinement, with both Japan and the ROK concentrating their resources on their near abroad, in particular within fragile states in Southeast Asia. The Philippines and the CLMV (Cambodia, Laos, Myanmar, and Vietnam) countries have been identified as containing within their borders the most "fragile" operating environments in the region, and therefore, have potentially the most to gain from partnering with nontraditional security and development entrepreneurs. Furthermore, this volume has highlighted that indeed, many of the human-centered policy initiatives emanating from Tokyo and Seoul have been operationalized within these countries, with significant benefits accruing to both sides in the partnerships.

At the level of central policy-making, Japan has explicitly mainstreamed human security into its development assistance programs aimed at Southeast Asian nations. Furthermore, Tokyo has targeted more refined niches within the development-peacebuilding-human-security nexus when engaging with challenges in the region. As highlighted in Chapter 4, these include efforts to combat human trafficking in the Mekong region in partnership with the CLMV countries (especially Myanmar and Vietnam) as well as Thailand, and support for peacebuilding in the Philippines (and also in Timor-Leste, the next most fragile operating environment according to the data in Chapter 3, although not explicitly addressed in Chapter 4).

Likewise, as detailed in Chapter 5, South Korea has implicitly mainstreamed human security through its emphasis on "humanitarianism" and, at both the policy level and that of public opinion, an awareness of the implications of "paying back" the international community for assistance previously received in times of trouble. Of South Korea's 26 priority development partners, the largest geographical concentration is in Asia (11 countries), with six in Southeast Asia, including the five fragile operating environments plus Indonesia. Focus sectors with priority partner countries which are also listed as fragile demonstrate a particular humanitarian leaning, including Cambodia (Rural and Agriculture Development/Green Energy/Human Resource Development/Health and Medical Care), Laos (Water Resources and Electricity/Human Resource Development/Health and Medical Care), Myanmar (Governance and Rural Development), Vietnam (Environment and Green Growth/Vocational Training), and the Philippines (Agriculture and Water

Resources/Health and Medical Care) (ODA Korea 2015). As also shown in Chapter 5, the ROK has supported humanitarian operations in all five of the fragile operating environments identified in Chapter 3. Furthermore, following the launch of the Mekong–ROK partnership in 2011, the Mekong–Korea Cooperation Fund (MKCF) was established in 2013 to encourage and support cooperation in six priority areas outlined in the 2011 Han River Declaration, including Green Growth and Human Resource Development, among all the CLMV countries plus Thailand (Mekong Institute n.d.).

Yet, while Chapters 4 and 5 have detailed some of the development and peacebuilding policy initiatives and implementations within Southeast Asian countries carried out by Japan and South Korea, there remains work to be done in terms of implementing a truly human-centric nontraditional security (NTS) agenda. Chapter 2 emphasized how the concept of human security has come to be seen as a connection between peacebuilding and development through highlighting local ownership or the "bottom-up" approach. Ishikawa and Howe note that when the perspective of human security is added to the discussion between peacebuilding and development, an emancipatory approach emerges, emphasizing local ownership, and only through such a "bottom-up" approach can a truly self-sustainable peace be built. The role of third parties or external actors is not eliminated, but rather the external actors need to enter a new partnership with local ownership. Likewise, in Chapter 3, Jang notes the importance of moving on from a focus on "fragile states" to one of "human fragility." The key factor running through all of the paradigms is the importance of human agency – peacebuilding from below, human development, and the notion of distributive justice, which emphasizes benefits to the least well-off and, of course, the prioritization of human rather than state security. While in their contributions to building peace and development in the region both Tokyo and Seoul have made considerable progress in this direction, where they can also both be criticized is in an ongoing focus on national interest and the needs of the state, whether in terms of external agent (donor) or regional development partner (recipient). This includes, in both cases, an ongoing reliance on a degree of tied aid rather than untied aid, on loans rather than grants, and on a unilateral soft power interpretation of public diplomacy, rather than multilateralism (Howe 2017a; Howe 2017b; OECD 2012; OECD 2014).

Nevertheless, despite strategic difficulties and internal and external constraints, Japan and South Korea have been making efforts to embrace more human-centered perspectives, in part because of the comparative advantages such approaches can bring to both parties. Even given the near universal acceptance of international governance norms revolving around the concepts of human security and the responsibility to protect (R2P), there remain significant discrepancies in how these norms are interpreted and operationalized. At the theoretical level, the fault lines are between narrow and broad interpretations of human security, the relationship between human security and the R2P, and the extent to which R2P is permissive of humanitarian intervention. At the level of practical policy implementation, these divergent approaches have been embodied in Western and Asian initiatives, including those of the most active and representative countries in their respective regions. Essentially the West holds a narrow view of human security, but an interventionary interpretation of R2P, with the two being closely linked, whereas in Asia, the linkage between the two is rejected, and a broad conceptualization of human security along with a noninterventionary understanding of the R2P dominates (Howe 2018, 80). As detailed in Chapter 2, Western "liberal peace" interpretations of peacebuilding can be seen as too interventionary in the Asian region, and, especially when related to regime change and democratic imposition aspirations, as even reaching the level of neo-imperialism.

The ROK is entirely free from any imperial or neo-imperial baggage, and, since the anti-Japanese riots of the 1970s in Southeast Asian capitals, Tokyo has successfully implemented policies to assuage their own imperial legacy. The Permanent Representative of South Korea to the UN stressed that "the primary responsibility lies in the individual Government while the international community bears the secondary responsibility," that R2P is "distinctly different from humanitarian intervention since it is based on collective actions, in accordance with UN Charter," and that "not all humanitarian tragedies or human rights violations can or should activate R2P" (Park 2009). For Japan, "while R2P recognizes the necessity for enforcement in certain circumstances, human security rules it out in every occasion"; therefore, the focus is one of prevention reducing the need for intervention (Bellamy and Davies 2009, 552). Partnerships with regional actors such as Japan and the ROK, which, although democracies and allies of the Western powers, still share a more "harmonious" noninterventionary perspective on human security, may, therefore, be more appealing to Southeast Asian countries.

This certainly seems to have been the case in terms of engagement and human security promotion in Myanmar through successive challenges to and opportunities for development and peacebuilding. Of all the challenges faced by the people of Myanmar, perhaps the gravest was the impact of Cyclone Nargis in May 2008. Cyclone Nargis was the deadliest ever faced by the country, and one of the most devastating storms recorded anywhere in the world. It officially killed more than 140,000 people, although some commentators put the death toll at over 300,000 (UNEP 2009, 3). Approximately 800,000 people were displaced, of whom 260,000 sought shelter in camps and settlements throughout the delta (*ibid.*). The government was accused of providing little relief assistance while at the same time hampering external aid (Özerdem 2010, 693). While Western actors were denied opportunities to help by the government of Myanmar, leading to some Western commentators calling for an "aid invasion," Asian actors were ultimately able to provide a leading role in assisting the people of Myanmar (Evans 2008; Howe 2018, 91; Kapucu 2011, 12).

Thus, addressing human fragility through local ownership actually represents a tremendous opportunity for proactive NTS policy-making for Japan and South Korea. Potential benefits of Japanese and Korean NTS policy platforms are not, however, limited to those that accrue to Tokyo and Seoul in terms of international prestige, soft power, and public diplomacy. Nor are they limited to the increased human security of vulnerable individuals and groups in fragile operating environments in Southeast Asia. Similar norm-internalization and policy-prioritization processes have opened up the possibility of "normalization" of engagement and cooperation between Japan and South Korea, and even a more peaceful regional operating environment.

Spillover

According to David Mitrany (1933, 101), collective governance and "material interdependence" develops its own internal dynamic as states integrate in limited functional, technical, and/or economic areas. This promotes a peaceful outlook among actors because everybody is made better off by cooperation, because economic interdependence increases the cost of war and the benefits of peace (*status quo*) and because cooperation "spills over" into the high political sphere of security through the establishment of a culture of cooperation rather than conflict. The English School rationalist perspective of an international society sheds light on the peacebuilding properties of international socialization and rule-construction in international organizations. English School rationalists examine and explain the behavior of states as being a product of socialization through repeated interactions with each other, which throw up common norms and principles to which all are inclined to adhere. Thus, the concept of an international "society" the rules and norms of which have a "civilizing" influence upon its members, rather than an international system governed by the logic of survival and self-help, is key to this perspective.

For Hedley Bull (1977, 13),

> a society of states (or international society) exists when a group of states, conscious of certain common interests and common values, form a society in the sense that they conceive themselves to be bound by a common set of rules in their relations with one another, and share in the working of common institutions.

Organizations create new internal cultures of interaction between states; "diplomatic culture" for Bull (*ibid.*, 316) is a system of norms and rules that is capable of constraining the violent behavior between states with diverse ambitions and cultures. Bull and Watson (1984, 1) are more explicit about the distinction between role of social norms and culture versus national interests of the members in the organization, noting that a group of independent political communities (states) can move beyond merely forming a system, "in the sense that the behavior of each is a necessary factor in the calculations of the others, to establishing, by dialogue and consent common rules and institutions for the conduct of their relations, and by recognizing their common interest in maintaining these arrangements." They also argue that "normative" and "institutional" factors create a unique "logic" for that particular international society (*ibid.*, 9). Thus, through mutual recognition not only of the shared domestic governance norms, but also of the simultaneous humanitarian internalization and directionality of foreign policy decision-making agendas, a more productive diplomatic culture can evolve between Tokyo and Seoul.

Furthermore, as humanitarian and pro-peace norms permeate through Japanese and Korean societies, when combined with the enhanced rolls of publics and civil societies in diplomatic output, there is greater potential to overcome the historical overhangs which have bedeviled relations between the two states. Karl Deutsch (1978, 119–22) refers to a simple cascade model of national decision-making consisting of five levels, each level a distinct reservoir of public or elite opinion and each reservoir linked to a complex of social institutions and status groups. The first of these is the social and economic elite, which does not form a simple monolithic group, but rather is connected by a dense net of multiple ties, links, and channels of communication. The second is the political and governmental elite, which is also not monolithic. Third we have the media of mass communication, fourth the network of local opinion leaders, and fifth the politically relevant strata of the population at large. Streams of information move downward in cascade fashion, from higher-level communications systems to lower-level ones.

In the contemporary operating environment, with heavy penetration of states by new media and high levels of personal contact between the peoples of different states, ideas and norms are now able to diffuse much more rapidly, and the directionality of the cascade could conceivably be reversed, or at the very least, be seen as operating in both directions. Hence, Nyan Chanda (2008, 307–9) notes that "New Preachers," NGOs and civil society community activists, have sprouted in many countries in the region to uphold humanitarian causes and to pressure governments and corporations, and that these activists have also linked with international bodies and fellow activists in other countries for coordination and support. Thus, for Nicholas Cull (2013, 17), "the significance of publics in foreign policy may be the defining characteristic of foreign policy in our age."

Essentially then, the jumping-off point is a view of the relationship between international operating environments and domestic constituencies as being one that is mutually constitutive. Increasingly, domestic constituencies are impacting on the normative framework of international relations, contributing to the construction of constraining rules and laws, but also introducing new agendas and opportunities. At the same time, the international normative operating environment is increasingly concerned with the rights, well-being, and security of vulnerable groups and individuals, even at the expense of state sovereignty and rights. Indeed, spillover can now be found not only between high politics and low politics, but also between international, national, and human security. In the contemporary operating environment, conflictual relationships can only be transformed, therefore, and a lasting peace built, through a holistic approach.

This social aspect of potential transformation of conflictual interstate relationships can be termed "socialization." Socialization is a process of inducting actors into the norms and rules of a given community, with compliance based on the internalization of these new norms. Thus, states, in adopting community rules associated with international organizations and institutions, switch from following the "logic of consequences to a logic of appropriateness; this adoption is sustained over time and is quite independent from a particular structure of material incentives or sanctions" (Checkel 2005, 804). The classical, sociological definition of socialization is "the process by which actors internalize the expectations of behavior imparted to them by the social environment" (Boekl, Rittberger, and Wagner 1999, 7). Finnemore and Sikkink (1998, 904) have pointed out how "state leaders conform to norms in order to avoid the disapproval aroused by norm violation and thus to enhance national esteem (and, as a result, their own self-esteem)." Thus, social norms which can be defined as "intersubjectively shared, value-based expectations of appropriate behavior" may serve as independent variables for explanations of foreign policy behavior (Boekl, Rittberger, and Wagner 1999, 4).

Finnemore and Sikkink (1998, 893–8) have also, therefore, pointed out the importance of the role of "norm entrepreneurs," further illustrating how "many international norms began as domestic norms and become international through the efforts of entrepreneurs of various kinds." They further note (2001, 393), "the most important ideational factors are widely shared or 'intersubjective' beliefs, which are not reducible to individuals." Likewise, for Risse, Ropp, and Sikkink (1999, 9), "[i]dentities then define the range of interests of actors considered as both possible and appropriate. Identities also provide a measure of inclusion and exclusion by defining a social 'we' and delineating the boundaries of the 'others.'"

Thus, from the top down, peace can be socially constructed through the socialization of states or their elites, or through a norm "cascade" or "spiral" model, whereby they permeate down through conflictual levels of society. On the other hand, norms related to peace and human security can permeate up from societies through national hierarchies, to the international operating environment through the activities of norm entrepreneurs. Policymakers and representatives in Japan and the ROK have the opportunity to behave in just such an entrepreneurial fashion. Furthermore, it is in their rational self-interest to do so, not just because peaceful regimes are beneficial to all, but also, because multilateralism and network diplomacy have come of age in the post–Cold War era.

Regional cooperation for peace and development

For Melissen (2005, 14), public diplomacy is neither an altruistic affair nor necessarily a "soft" instrument, as it can

> pursue a wide variety of objectives, such as in the field of political dialogue, trade and foreign investment, the establishment of links with civil society groups beyond the opinion gatekeepers, but also has "hard power" goals such as alliance management, conflict prevention or military intervention.

This combination of hard power and soft power in the contemporary discourse is termed "smart power," and this seems an apt description of the policy direction successive administrations in both Tokyo and Seoul have chosen to pursue in order to increase their system-affecting status. Yet, the current prioritization by Japan and South Korea of unilateral niche diplomacy and bilateral partnerships, as well a focus on soft power and influence rather than the power of attraction, may not in fact be the best way to maximize this influence.

Melissen's "new" conceptualization of public diplomacy moves away from soft power promotion, the "peddling" of information to foreigners and "keeping the foreign press at bay, toward engaging with foreign audiences" (Melissen 2005, 4). Thus, Brian Hocking (2005, 29) contrasts two different models of public diplomacy: a state-centered, hierarchical model in which renewed emphasis is given to public diplomacy within the traditional image of intergovernmental relations, and a new "network" model of diplomacy. The network model of public diplomacy is increasingly defined as diplomacy "by" rather than "of" publics through which individuals and groups, "empowered by the resources provided by the CIT revolution . . . are direct participants in the shaping of international policy and, through an emergent global civil society, may operate through or independently of national governments" (Hocking 2005, 29). It thus provides a "fundamentally different picture of how diplomacy works in the twenty-first century and, thereby, the significance of its public (as well as its private) dimension" (Hocking 2005, 37). For Rudderham (2008, 2), "middle power states have most recently been defined by their internationalism. States that exhibit certain foreign policy behavior are considered middle powers. Qualifying behavior might include good 'global citizenship,' niche diplomacy, and accepting roles as mediators, followers, or staunch multilateralists."

From this perspective, status as a middle power is conferred in accordance with behavior rather than size. Middle power activism is all about visibility on the international stage, but it is also about playing by the rules of the global normative consensus and demonstrating a willingness to be a good global citizen. In the new "networked" operating environment of public diplomacy, multilateralism plays a bigger role than ever before. Multilateralism encourages the formation, maintenance, and use of networks of social, cultural, political, and economic connections within and between actors as a method of persuasion in public diplomacy (Rudderham 2008, 6). The networking role of middle powers is amplified under the current architecture of global governance featuring multiple channels for expression such as the UN, the Organization of Economic Cooperation and Development (OECD), the World Bank, the Group of Twenty (G20), the World Trade Organization (WTO), and the proliferation of regional organizations. Jordaan (2013, 169) argues that the preference among contemporary middle powers for internationalism and multilateralism arises "from the inability of these states to unilaterally and single-handedly shape global outcomes in any direct manner." Multilateral settings and the liberal norms they advocate provide a platform to ensure that the voices of middle powers are not neglected by the major powers (Teo, Singh, and Tan 2013).

Here, the overt pursuit of national interest is even further removed, with a role more akin to international public servant and good global citizen being presented to the world by the middle power concerned. Actions range from the "good offices" function of hosting international organizations, summits, and other meetings, through the agenda setting of chairing such meetings and the bridging role between contentious parties, to direct contributions to the global commons. In carrying out these functions in an apparently altruistic manner, the middle power gains significant reputational resources which can be channeled through other avenues of public diplomacy. It is possible for a country to do well by doing good: supporting "good" works, performing "good" deeds, using "good" words, projecting "good" images, and hosting "good" institutions can pay off in terms of international prestige and the appreciation of others. "A country can become known, admired, and also rewarded for its 'goodness' – which becomes a kind of niche in itself" (Henrikson 2005, 68).

As detailed in Chapters 4 and 5, both Japan and South Korea have taken note of the importance of multilateralism. Japan has been at the forefront of international efforts to institutionalize the pursuit of human security at the UN and related institutions. Meanwhile, South Korea has hosted the G20, the High-Level Forum (HLF-4) on Aid Effectiveness, and is home to the Global Green Growth Institute (GGGI), a treaty-based international organization headquartered in Seoul, which pursues "strategies that simultaneously achieve poverty reduction, social inclusion, environmental sustainability, and economic growth" (GGGI n.d.). Country programs supported by the GGGI are in place in all five of the fragile operating environments identified in Chapter 2. Both countries have also been active in multilateral institution-building in Southeast Asia.

Japan was at the forefront of moves to establish Asia-Pacific Economic Cooperation (APEC), the Asia Development Bank (ADB), East Asian Community, ASEAN Plus Three, the East Asia Summit (EAS), the Six-Party Talks, and Economic Partnership Agreements with ASEAN countries and the ROK. Japan is the largest supporter of the ADB and has always held the presidency, and Japan continues to be the biggest trading partner, investing country, and Official Development Assistance (ODA) donor for ASEAN. Japan has also been particularly supportive in political and economic terms of the process of ASEAN integration, facilitating the construction of a zone of peace within which freedom from fear has been considerably enhanced, and as a result of which a peace dividend has been generated and win-win economic cooperation encouraged (Yoshimatsu and Trinidad 2010). JICA has partnered with the ASEAN Institutes of Strategic and International Studies (ASEAN-ISIS) and the ASEAN People's Assembly (APA) to develop a people-centered ASEAN.

South Korea has been participating actively in regional multilateralism and is especially committed to ASEAN institution- and community-building efforts (Teo, Singh, and Tan 2013; Mo 2016). The ROK has also assumed a leadership role in attempted regionalization initiatives. The inauguration of East Asia Summit (EAS) in 2005 was led by former Korean President Kim Dae-jung's initiative on the establishment of the East Asian Vision Group (EAVG) in 1998 that grew out of the experience of the 1997 financial crisis (Teo, Singh, and Tan 2013). Seoul has been involved in all the major ASEAN-led dialogue platforms such as the ASEAN Plus Three (APT), ASEAN Regional Forum (ARF), ASEAN Defense Minister's Meeting-Plus (ADMM-Plus), and East Asia Summit (EAS). As mentioned in Chapter 5,

South Korea has also taken a regional cooperative view on development cooperation through the ASEAN-ROK cooperation fund.

Multilateral collaboration between these two middle powers, with similar interests, political culture, and outlooks, remains limited, however. They of course work together in the multilateral fora detailed above. There has also been a degree of collaboration between the government agencies of JICA and KOICA; between their academic counterparts, the JICA Research Institute (JICA-RA), the Korean Association of International Development and Cooperation (KAIDEC), and other bodies; and during some UN-led peace-keeping operations. Yet perhaps due to a combination of historical over-hangs, lack of awareness or understanding of the "other," and perceptions of the pursuit of national interest being of necessity zero-sum, many potential collective gains (for both the Northeast Asian actors and their Southeast Asian partners) have been "left on the table."

Conclusion

This volume, therefore, has sought to highlight the synergy of interests, not only between Northeast Asian actors and their Southeast Asian partners, but also between Japan and South Korea themselves. The processes of making foreign policy decisions and forming assumptions about the nature of the "other" comprise major challenges to the transformation of conflictual relationships and construction of an enduring peace in Northeast Asia, as well as the attempts at peacebuilding in Southeast Asian fragile operating environments addressed in the other chapters of this book. The biggest obstacles to the normalization of relations between two like-minded polities such as Japan and South Korea do not revolve around a lack of shared interest, but rather a lack of awareness of shared interests, a lack of understanding of the "other" and therefore a lack of trust, and misperceptions about the others' interests, intents, and actions. The socialization processes discussed above (in the section titled Spillover), through which repeated interaction can play a major role in communication-based relationship building, are key to overcoming these challenges.

Theorists such as Roger Fisher (Fisher, Ury, and Patton 1991; Fisher et al. 1997) and John Burton (1969, 1990a, 1990b) have tried to formalize and model this process. The first step is to assess our own assumptions about the other, the nature of our conflictual relationship with them, and the data upon which we base them (sometimes called "assessing the first position"). Next, it is important to "assess the second position:" consider what the other parties see (their partisan perceptions), why they see it that way (their back-ground, emotions, and motives), and the interests which lie behind their positions (Fisher et al. 1997, 48–51). In other words, what are our assumptions, why do we make them, is there any evidence that does not support our

A. Assumptions	B. Base Data
What are the core assumptions about the conflict?	*On what data have the assumptions been based?*
D. Alternative Assumptions	C. Nonconforming Data
Taking the additional data into account, what might be some alternative conclusions about the conflict?	*What additional data might be considered that may be inconsistent with the core assumptions?*

Figure 6.1 The assumptions/data tool

assumptions, and are there alternative explanations for our perceived reality which may fit the available data equally well or even better (Howe 2016, 8)? This has been modeled by the Assumptions/Data Tool shown in Figure 6.1. The third step is to interact with the other parties in order to test our understanding of their positions. Parties engage in "active listening" whereby the positions and underlying interests of other actors are directly solicited.

Hence, communication and interaction form the bedrock of improved relationships, which for Fisher et al. (1991) is an important strategic objective in its own right, independent of the pursuit of each actor's individual interest satisfaction. For followers of John Burton, the process has tended to involve a problem-solving workshop to which all parties with the capacity to affect the outcome of negotiations are invited, where their common problems are jointly addressed as collective action rather than adversarial zero-sum negotiations. This inclusive approach means including non-state actors as participants. It also uses non-state actors in key organizational roles due to their nonconfrontational and non-zero-sum positioning. For instance, the workshop is often organized and held by academics in a university seminar setting. In the workshop, each party must explain the other's position to the satisfaction of the other (Burton 1969). In the fourth and final step, given this new understanding, rather than focusing on how to achieve our own goals, we consider whether there are other ways in which we can ensure the substantive interests (not positions) of the other party, with the aim of a more lasting settlement and maintenance of a long-term cooperative relationship.

Thus, collaboration on this volume has served two purposes in relation to building relationships as a step toward normalizing interactions between Japan and South Korea. First, in terms of output, it has drawn attention to the shared interests and commonalities of purpose for the two middle powers. Second, in terms of soliciting contributions from scholars and practitioners of development and peacebuilding who are connected with the main policy-making and academic institutions of the two countries, it has promoted the socialization agenda between potential norm entrepreneurs in Japan and the ROK. It is to be hoped that the authors, as well as the readers of this book, will strive for greater collaboration between Japan and South Korea in the promotion of peace and development in fragile operating environments in Southeast Asia for the greater good not only of vulnerable individuals and groups, but also for the aspiration of building a humanitarian-focused normative regional community.

References

Bellamy, A. J. and Davies, S. E. (2009) "The responsibility to protect in the Asia-Pacific region" *Security Dialogue* 40(6) 547–74.

Boekl, H., Rittberger, V., and Wagner, W. (1999) *Norms and Foreign Policy: Constructivist Foreign Policy Analysis* University of Tubingen Press, Tubingen.

Bull, H. (1977) *The Anarchical Society: A Study of Order in World Politics* Macmillan, London.

Bull, H. and Watson, A. (1984) *The Expansion of International Society* Oxford University Press, Oxford.

Burton, J. W. (1969) *Conflict and Communication* Macmillan, London.

——— (1990a) *Conflict: Resolution and Prevention* St. Martin's Press, New York.

——— (1990b) *Conflict: Human Needs Theory* St. Martin's Press, New York.

Calder, K. (1988) "Japanese foreign economic policy formation: Explaining the reactive state" *World Politics* 40(4) 517–41.

Chanda, N. (2008) "Globalization and international politics in Asia" in Shambaugh, D. and Yahuda, M. eds., *International Relations of Asia* Rowman & Littlefield, Plymouth.

Checkel, J. (2005) "International institutions and socialization in Europe: Introduction and framework" *International Organization* 59(4) 801–26.

Cull, N. (2013) "Issue brief: 'Bulging ideas:' Making Korean public diplomacy work" *Public Diplomacy Magazine* Summer (http://publicdiplomacymagazine.com/issue-brief-bulging-ideas-making-korean-public-diplomacy-work/) Accessed July 23, 2018.

Deutsch, K. (1978) *The Analysis of International Relations* 2nd Edition Prentice-Hall, Englewood Cliffs, NJ.

Evans, G. (2008) "Time for an aid invasion?" *The Age* May 19 (www.theage.com.au/news/opinion/time-for-an-aidinvasion/2008/05/18/1211049061508.html) Accessed July 23, 2018.

Finnemore, M. and Sikkink, K. (1998) "International norm dynamics and political change" *International Organization* 52 887–917.

——— (2001) "Taking stock: The constructivist research program in international relations and comparative politics" *Annual Review of Political Science* 4 391–416.

Fisher, R., Schneider, A. K., Bogwardt, E., and Ganson, B. (1997) *Coping with International Conflict* Prentice-Hall, Englewood Cliffs, NJ.

Fisher, R., Ury, W., and Patton, B. (1991) *Getting to Yes* Penguin, New York.

Frances, J. (2017) "In the firing line: South Korea's wartime OPCOM transfer" *Foreign Brief* November 7 (www.foreignbrief.com/asia-pacific/firing-line-south-korea-opcon-transfer/) Accessed July 23, 2018.

GGGI (Global Green Growth Institute), n.d. http://gggi.org/about/ Accessed July 27, 2018.

Henrikson, A. (2005) "Niche diplomacy in the world public arena: The global 'corners' of Canada and Norway" in Melissen, J. ed., *The New Public Diplomacy: Soft Power in International Relations* Palgrave Macmillan, Basingstoke 67–87.

Hirata, K. (1998) "Japan as a reactivist state? Analyzing Japan's relations with the Socialist Republic of Vietnam" *Japanese Studies* 18(2) 1–31.

Hocking, B. (2005) "Rethinking the 'new' public diplomacy" in Melissen, J. ed., *The New Public Diplomacy: Soft Power in International Relations* Palgrave Macmillan, Basingstoke 28–46.

Howe, B. (2016) "Building enduring peace in Northeast Asia: Overcoming perceptional and positional obstacles" *Asian Journal of Peacebuilding* 4(1) 1–23.

——— (2017a) "Korea's role for peace-building and development in Asia" *Asian Journal of Peacebuilding* 5(2) 243–66.

——— (2017b) "Challenges and opportunities for South Korean diplomacy in an era of new varieties of power and influence" *Korean Journal of Security Affairs* 22(1) 4–22.

——— (2018) "Divergent interpretations of the R2P and human security: Implications for governance challenges in Myanmar" *Korean Journal of Security Affairs* 23(1) 80–101.

Jordaan, E. (2013) "The concept of a middle power in international relations: Distinguishing between emerging and traditional middle powers" *South African Journal of Political Studies* 30(1) 165–81.

Kapucu, N. (2011) "Collaborative governance in international disasters: Nargis Cyclone in Myanmar and Sichuan earthquake in China cases" *International Journal of Emergency Management* 8(1) 1–25.

Mekong Institute, n.d. "Mekong: ROK Cooperation Fund" (www.mekonginstitute.org/what-we-do/development-funds/mekong-rok-cooperation-fund/) Accessed July 25, 2018.

Melissen, J. (2005) "The new public diplomacy: Between theory and practice" in Melissen, J. ed., *The New Public Diplomacy: Soft Power in International Relations* Palgrave Macmillan, Basingstoke 3–27.

Mitrany, D. (1933) *The Progress of International Government* Yale University Press, New Haven.

Mo, J. (2016) "South Korea's middle power diplomacy: A case of growing compatibility between regional and global roles" *International Journal* 71(4) 587–607.

ODA Korea (2015) "Country partnership strategy" (www.odakorea.go.kr/eng.policy.CountryPartnershipStrategy.do) Accessed July 25, 2018.

OECD (Organisation for Economic Cooperation and Development) (2012) "Korea: Development Assistance Committee (DAC) peer review 2012" (www.oecd.org/dac/peer-reviews/Korea%20CRC%20-%20FINAL%2021%20JAN.pdf) Accessed July 20, 2018.

———— (2014) "Japan: DAC peer reviews of development co-operation, 2014" (www.oecd.org/dac/peer-reviews/peer-review-japan.htm) Accessed July 23, 2018.

Özerdem, A. (2010) "The 'responsibility to protect' in natural disasters: Another excuse for interventionism? Nargis Cyclone, Myanmar" *Conflict, Security & Development* 10(5) 693–713.

Park, I. K. (2009) "Statement by H. E. Mr. Park In-kook, permanent representative of the Republic of Korea to the United Nations, plenary meeting of the General Assembly on responsibility to protect" July 23 (www.responsibilitytoprotect.org/Korea_ENG.pdf.) Accessed July 23, 2018.

Risse, T., Ropp, S. C., and Sikkink, K. (1999) *The Power of Human Rights: International Norms and Domestic Change* Cambridge University Press, Cambridge.

Rudderham, M. A. (2008) "Middle power pull: Can middle powers use public diplomacy to ameliorate the image of the West?" *YCISS Working Paper No. 46* February.

Teo, S., Singh, B., and Tan, S. (2013) "South Korea's middle-power engagement initiatives: Perspectives from Southeast Asia" *RSIS Working Paper No. 265* Nanyang Technological University, Singapore (https://dr.ntu.edu.sg/bitstream/handle/10220/20083/WP265.pdf?sequence=1) Accessed July 27, 2018.

UNEP (United Nations Environment Programme) (2009) "Learning from Cyclone Nargis: Investing in the environment for livelihoods and disaster risk reduction" (http://wedocs.unep.org/handle/20.500.11822/14116) Accessed July 23, 2018.

Yoshimatsu, H. and Trinidad, F. (2010) "Development assistance, strategic interests, and the China factor in Japan's role in ASEAN integration" *Japanese Journal of Political Science* 11(2) 199–219.

Index